the
indy 500

FRANKLIN WATTS
A Division of Scholastic Inc.
New York • Toronto • London • Auckland • Sydney
Mexico City • New Delhi • Hong Kong
Danbury, Connecticut

MARK STEWART

Researched and Edited by
MIKE KENNEDY

Cover design by Dave Klaboe   Series design by Molly Heron

Cover photo IDs: (center) 1976 Indy 500 official program; (clockwise from upper left) Race car driver, Arie Luyendyk; A.J. Foyt representing Goodyear on the cover of *Auto Racing Digest*; A collector's Cummins Diesel trading card; Mario Andretti during a 1965 race; Al Unser Jr. gracing the cover of *Racing Monthly*; 1966 pace car; Janet Guthrie, the first woman to ever enter the Indy 500; Parnelli Jones speeding around the track.

Photographs © 2003: AP/Wide World Photos: 79 (Mark Duncan), 60 (Charles A. Robinson), 22, 34; Courtesy of Indianapolis Motor Speedway/IMS Properties, Inc.: 76 (Leigh Spargur), 4, 6, 9, 15, 16, 18, 19, 20 top, 20 bottom, 21, 23, 25, 26, 29, 30, 36, 41, 44, 45, 46, 47, 48, 56, 58, 59, 62 right, 62 left, 63, 64, 65 bottom, 65 top, 66, 69, 70, 74, 75, 77, 78 bottom, 78 top, 80, 81, 87, 90; Team Stewart, Inc.: all cover photos.

Library of Congress Cataloging-in-Publication Data

Stewart, Mark.
    The Indy 500 / Mark Stewart.
        p. cm. — (The Watts history of sports)
    Includes bibliographical references and index.
    Summary: Looks at the history of the oldest and most famous automobile
    race in the United States, run each year since 1911 on Memorial Day
    Weekend at the Indianapolis Motor Speedway.
    ISBN 0-531-11954-8
    1. Indianapolis Speedway Race—Juvenile literature.
    [1. Indianapolis Speedway Race. 2.(Automobile racing.) I. Title: Indy Five Hundred.
    II. Kennedy, Mike (Mike William), 1965- III. Title. IV. Series.
    GV1033.5.I55S84 2003
    796.72'09772'52—dc21   2003005813

CONTENTS

The Indianapolis Motor Speedway as it looks today.

INTRODUCTION

Incredible as it may seem, in the early years of the 20th century, many Americans thought the automobile was little more than a smelly, noisy, dangerous "passing fad." Carl Fisher was not among these non-believers. The owner of the Indianapolis-based Prest-O-Lite company, which made carbide headlamps for motor cars, Fisher not only saw a bright future for the automotive business, he aimed to make his hometown the heart of the industry.

Fisher was one of several automotive pioneers who lived in Indiana. Arthur Newby of National Motors and Frank Wheeler of Wheeler-Schebler Carburetor believed—as Fisher and Prest-O-Lite co-owner Jim Allison did—that the best way to convince the rest of the nation that Indianapolis was the cradle of the car business was to hold the nation's biggest race.

Fisher and his partners set about the task of building the country's most magnificent oval track—2.5 miles long with four corners banked at 9 degrees. The Indianapolis Motor Speedway opened on August 19, 1909. The first race held on the track demonstrated the high speeds that could be attained on the track, but also exposed dangerous flaws in its design. The combination of fast cars and heat caused the original crushed stone and tar surface to break up. Five people died as a result.

Fisher, facing possible financial ruin, could have cut his losses and abandoned his dream. Instead, he responded by tearing up the track and laying 3.2 million 10-pound bricks, grouted with cement, to form an entirely new and highly durable surface. Fisher reopened the track in December to rave reviews. The first winner on the new track was named Louis Strang, and he drove a Fiat to victory.

In 1910, three, three-day festivals were held at the "Brickyard," featuring dozens of races between all types of cars at a number of different distances. These events proved very popular with fans, drivers, and auto designers. After the final 1910 event, held on Labor Day, Fisher and his partners announced that henceforth the Speedway would host one race a year, over Memorial Day weekend: The Indianapolis 500 International Sweepstakes.

In order to lure the top drivers and generate media attention, Fisher made his "Indy 500" the highest-paying sporting event in America. It was a stroke of genius. Drivers knew they could gain national fame by doing well and car-builders knew their innovations would get tremendous press coverage if they proved worthy.

From the first race the Indy 500 took on a life of its own. Each year after that, an exciting new chapter was added to the longest and most fascinating racing story in North America.

There is no scene in racing like Pit Row at Indy. Here more than a dozen competitors pull in for repairs and refueling during the 2002 race.

CHAPTER 1

THE EARLY YEARS

1911

Fans expecting an unprecedented spectacle were not disappointed by the first Indy 500. With a record-setting purse of $27,550, the event attracted a qualifying field of 46 cars from the U.S. and Europe. Any car that could sustain a speed of 75 mph was permitted to join the starting field; all but six vehicles made it. The list of drivers competing in this historic race included such luminaries as Ralph Mulford, Johnny Aitken, Spencer Wishart, David Bruce-Brown, and reigning AAA champion Ray Harroun, who came out of retirement to get in on the action.

Carl Fisher drove the pace car for the first lap, then pulled off the track as the competitors roared past him. In the race's early stages, Aitken zoomed to the lead in his National. Then Wishart took control in his Mercedes until Bruce-Brown's Fiat surged ahead. All the while, Mulford and Harroun stayed within striking distance of the leaders. Harroun's strong showing was a surprise to many. Not only was he piloting a self-built yellow-and-black Marmon "Wasp," he was driving solo. In the days before pit crews, racing cars typically had a driver and a mechanic. Sometimes the "riding mechanic" would crawl out on the hood and make repairs while the car was still in motion.

Harroun decided to go it alone. Without a passenger, however, he had no one to check on the action behind him. He installed rearview mirrors, which were considered revolutionary at the time. As Harroun moved up on the leaders and then overtook them, Mulford stayed in his rearview.

With 64 laps remaining, Harroun wobbled into the pit area to change a blown tire. Mulford moved in front, but his Lozier soon required repairs of its own. Harroun reassumed command (the seventh lead change of the day) then held on to take the checkered flag. In all, 26 of 40 entrants finished the race. The only fatality occurred on the 12th lap, when Arthur Greiner's Amplex slammed into the wall and his mechanic, Sam Dickson, was thrown to his death. Unfortunately, seatbelts were still many years away.

Winner: Ray Harroun
Car: Marmon
Average Speed: 74.60 mph
  2. Ralph Mulford
  3. David Bruce-Brown
  4. Spencer Wishart
  5. Joe Dawson

1912

The second Indy 500 featured a smaller field (24 cars), but that did not diminish the excitement. More than 80,000 fans gathered at the Brickyard to watch a field that included Joe Dawson, Ralph DePalma, Hughie Hughes, Ralph Mulford, Eddie Rickenbacker, Teddy Tetzlaff, and David Bruce-Brown, the fastest qualifier at 88.45 mph. Going into the 1912 event, track officials instituted several new rules. First, all drivers were required to race with a riding mechanic, which meant no more "single-seaters." Second, only those cars that completed all 500 miles would be eligible to collect prize money.

Tetzlaff flew into the lead at the start, but three laps into the race DePalma edged his way to the front. Dawson, driving a blue and white National, settled in behind DePalma. For a good part of the day, these drivers raced one-two. DePalma built a two-lap lead with just three laps to go, when suddenly his car came to a stop, the victim of a bad connector rod. He and his riding mechanic, Rupert Jeffkins, leaped from their white Mercedes and pushed it into the pits, where they worked feverishly to repair the damage. Dawson, 10 minutes ahead of the third-place Fiat being driven by Tetzlaff, made up the laps he needed and cruised to victory unchallenged. DePalma never got his car going again, and therefore did not collect a dime for his efforts.

In a bizarre footnote, the race did not end for several more hours. Mulford, who had been quarreling with track officials ever since the 1911 event, decided to get some revenge. Because of the mandatory finishing rule, he knew no one could go home until he completed all 200 laps. After Dawson took the checkered flag, Mulford slowed his Knox to a pace more suited to a leisurely Sunday drive.

As Fisher and his partners watched in frustration, Mulford circled the track in low gear—and even stopped along the way to consume a dinner of fried chicken and ice cream! When he finally crossed the finish line, the race was six hours old; his average speed of 56.3 mph is still the lowest in Indy 500 history.

> **Winner: Joe Dawson**
> **Car: National**
> **Average Speed: 78.7 mph**
>   2. **Teddy Tetzlaff**
>   3. **Hughie Hughes**
>   4. **Charlie Merz**
>   5. **Bill Endicott**

1913

Racing fans suspected that it would only be a matter of time before the Midwest's unpredictable spring weather would play a role in the 500. On race day in 1913, it was 90 degrees in the shade. This would cause the 27 qualifiers a lot of extra headaches, as the sun beat down on the track throughout the race. Among those assembled in the starting grid were Ralph DePalma, Charlie Merz, Ralph Mulford, Spencer Wishart, and Jack Tower—each of whom was counted among the race favorites. Also in the field were a couple of French Peugeots, driven by Paul Zuccarelli and Jules Goux. Engine specifications had been loosened up in the hope of attracting more European cars and stars to the race. Goux and Zuccarelli were among the best wheel men in the world. Their cars were powered by four-cylinder engines with domed combustion chambers and dual overhead camshafts—features still used in modern engines.

The race started and the cars roared past the brand new, five-story timing and scoring tower. Goux sprinted into the lead, and held it with a clever bit of strategy. Sensing that the hot track would chew up everyone's tires, he coasted through the turns (which caused the most wear) and then stomped down on the accelerator when he reached the straightaways. His powerful Peugeot offered more than enough speed to win; all Goux needed to do was survive the withering heat. At all six of his refueling stops, he swigged on bottles of champagne. Goux probably sweated out the alcohol soon after he consumed it, otherwise he would have been weaving all over the track!

Other teams did not handle the heat as well. Countless blown tires had to be changed, and every other driver in the race had to be relieved by a substitute at one time or another. Goux carried the day, outdistancing Wishart's Mercer by a whopping 13 minutes. As the crowd waited for the others to complete the 200 laps (only 10 did), they witnessed an incredibly brave act by Merz's mechanic. With his Stutz heading for third place and a nice payday, an engine fire started. Harry Martin climbed onto the hood with the car still speeding along, and managed to extinguish the flames without losing ground to fast-closing Albert Guyot, who had to settle for fourth place.

> **Winner: Jules Goux**
> Car: Peugeot
> Average Speed: 75.9 mph
>   2. Spencer Wishart
>   3. Charlie Merz
>   4. Albert Guyot
>   5. Theodore Pilette

1914

The success of Jules Goux and his Peugeot in 1913 attracted several top Europeans to the 1914 Indy 500. Their cars, which were powered by lighter, more efficient engines than the American entries, had a distinct advantage. This was evident in qualifying, when Georges Boillot set a new record with a speed of just under 100 mph. Fifteen other cars eclipsed David Bruce-Brown's old mark. Boillot became the instant favorite, along with fellow Frenchmen, Goux, Arthur Duray, and Rene Thomas. Among the leading American drivers were Joe Dawson, Ray Gilhooley, Ralph Mulford, Barney Oldfield, Eddie Rickenbacker, Teddy Tetzlaff, and Howdy Wilcox.

The crowd of 100,000 cheered as Wilcox took an early lead, but his Gray Fox would not survive the day. Another top

Jules Goux, the first "rookie" winner of the 500, poses behind the wheel of his powerful Peugeot.

American, Gilhooley, lost his concentration on Lap 41 and tried a particularly bone-headed maneuver that resulted in his Isotta flipping over. From that day on, whenever a driver made a dumb mistake, Indy fans would say he "pulled a real Gilhooley."

As everyone anticipated, this race belonged to the French. Boillot, Thomas, and Duray established themselves as the men to beat, with Thomas's Delage in front for more than half the race. A blown tire and broken frame finished Boillot, and Duray's Peugeot—with the smallest engine in the race—just could not keep up. Thomas won easily, while three of his countrymen finished behind him. Oldfield, a legendary "speed demon" who earned his living giving exhibitions around the country, was the fastest American, finishing fifth.

Although Thomas won fair and square, American car-makers took heart in the knowledge that they might have beaten the French were it not for a pre-race mishap. Hughie Hughes had arrived in Indianapolis with a wondrously advanced six-cylinder engine. In practice runs, he was tearing around the track. However, prior to qualifying, Hughes was showing off to a female fan and over-revved the engine. The crankcase cracked and the car never again saw the light of day.

> **Winner: Rene Thomas**
> Car: Delage
> Speed: 82.5 mph
>   2. Arthur Duray
>   3. Albert Guyot
>   4. Jules Goux
>   5. Barney Oldfield

1915

Bad weather played havoc with the 1915 Indy 500, as torrential rains on race day postponed the start. The next day the weather was fine, but things had to dry out at least 24 hours before the race could be safely run. As many as 100,000 people had traveled to Indianapolis to watch the 500, and now something had to be done with them. There was not an empty bed in town, and stores and restaurants had run out of food. The thought of this army of tired, hungry racing fans with nothing to do on a sunny Sunday panicked the city fathers, who feared that rioting would break out. Carl Fisher came to the rescue. He staged a race between famous aviator DeLloyd Thompson's biplane and a Stutz driven by Barney Oldfield, which kept the crowd entertained. Ralph DePalma and other drivers pitched in, staging tire-changing contests and other impromptu competitions.

The fans moved to the speedway the next day expecting a fast race. New qualifying rules were in effect that seemed to ensure this. Only one car for every 400 feet of track would be allowed (a standard rule at most other American closed-track auto races) and no qualifier under 80 mph would make the starting field. A total of 33 cars could have made the cut, but only 24 did. And they were all good ones. Dario Resta's Peugeot was among the fastest in the race, and the Italian superstar (who was a British citizen) was a formidable driver. He was clearly the man to beat, along with Americans DePalma and Howdy Wilcox, who had turned in magnificent qualifying times. Absent from the field were the flying Frenchmen. War had erupted in Europe a few months after the 1914 race, and France was fighting for its life.

The race quickly turned into a duel between DePalma and Resta—two great drivers in two exceptional cars—with Earl Cooper and Gil Anderson trailing in their Stutzes, waiting for an opportunity to take the lead. That opportunity never came. De-Palma (who was better in the turns) gained an advantage over Resta (who made up ground in the straightaways) when Resta blew a tire on Lap 137. Resta returned to the track quickly and clung to second place. With three laps remaining, however, DePalma's engine began to fail. Luckily, he had a large enough lead to slow down and still finish first; his red-beige-and-black Mercedes was able to chug the last few miles without seizing. Even so, De-Palma broke the average speed record by a good 7 mph.

Winner: Ralph DePalma
Car: Mercedes
Speed: 89.8 mph
　　2. Dario Resta
　　3. Gil Anderson
　　4. Earl Cooper
　　5. Eddie O'Donnell

1916

In the spring of 1916, the United States had not officially entered the military conflict raging across the Atlantic. Yet many of the American manufacturers that had been concentrating their energies on the automotive business were now focused on producing items needed by England, France, and Italy

GREAT DRIVER: RALPH DEPALMA

America's first auto racing superstar was Ralph DePalma. He could drive any type of car to victory on any type of surface. Born in Italy and raised in New York, DePalma loved to race. He started as a high-school sprinter, moved to bicycle racing, then to motorcycles. In 1904, at the age of 21, he attended the Vanderbilt Cup auto race on Long Island and knew that this was what he wanted to do. By 1908, he was winning races and making a name for himself. He also started a long rivalry with Barney Oldfield, America's best known racer at the time.

In 1912, DePalma earned the admiration of fans when misfortune robbed him of victory at Indy with a lap and a half to go. The sight of DePalma and his mechanic trying to push their broken car into the pits before Joe Dawson swept past them is one of the most enduring stories from the early years of racing. Later that year, he won the AAA national championship; he repeated as champ in 1914. By 1915, when he finally won at Indy, DePalma was already a folk hero.

After retiring, DePalma stayed close to the racing business. He built and tested stock cars in the 1930s, setting numerous records in the process. Later, he became an honorary referee at the Speedway. In all, DePalma probably won over 2,000 automobile races in his career. His last came in 1929, at the age of 46.

for the war. Some companies reduced their racing programs to one or two cars, while others dropped out of the sport altogether. This accounted for the small qualifying field for the Indy 500 (just 30 cars) as well as the limited number of cars that actually made the cut (just 21)—and why the length of the race was reduced for the first and only time to 300 miles.

It did not account, however, for the absence of the defending champion, Ralph De-Palma. That was his own doing. Knowing Carl Fisher and his partners were worried that a diminished race might mean a diminished crowd, the 1915 winner demanded an appearance fee just to show up for the 1916 race. A DePalma-Resta rematch, he reasoned, could pull in many thousands who might otherwise choose to stay away. Fisher held his ground. He knew that paying De-Palma would open a door that might not be easy to close. His bluff called, DePalma agreed to enter the race. The clever Fisher pointed out that his application would now be two days late—and barred him from the competition! From that day on, there was little question as to who was the boss at Indy.

Without anyone to challenge Resta, he roared to an easy victory. Johnny Aitken stayed close for more than half the race, but his car dropped a valve and had to retire. Eddie Rickenbacker, who would soon become America's most famous flying ace in World War I, dropped out after just nine laps, his steering shot. Competing in their first 500, the Chevrolet brothers, Louis and Arthur, also failed to finish. That left Wilbur D'Alene and Ralph Mulford to chase Resta, who completed the 120 laps with just one pit stop. A crowd of 80,000 cheered him across the finish line, two minutes ahead of his pursuers.

Winner: Dario Resta
Car: Peugeot
Speed: 83.3 mph
  2. Wilbur D'Alene
  3. Ralph Mulford
  4. Josef Christiaens
  5. Barney Oldfield

CHAPTER 2

BETWEEN THE WARS

1919

America entered World War I in 1917 and fought through most of 1918. The Indianapolis Motor Speedway fell quiet for those two years, but in 1919 the race was on again. Much had been learned about engines during the war, particularly from aircraft, which demanded a maximum of power and a minimum of weight. By May, many of these lessons had been applied to racing cars, and fans were electrified when speeds at the Brickyard topped 100 mph in qualifying. Driving a Ballot, 1914 champion Rene Thomas turned in the fastest speed, 104.8 mph. Right behind him was Louis Chevrolet, in a Frontenac, at 103.1. Among the other race favorites were Louis's brother Gaston, along with Joe Boyer, Ralph DePalma, Jules Goux, Ralph Mulford, and Howdy Wilcox.

DePalma grabbed the lead early, and managed to keep his Packard ahead of the field for most of the first 100 laps. When he encountered wheel bearing problems in the second half of the race, he began to drop back, and Thomas surged into the lead. The Frenchman's time in front was short-lived, as he was plagued with mechanical troubles. Next came the trio of Wilcox, Goux,

and Eddie Hearne. Wilcox, a native of Indiana, was driving a Peugeot that was owned by the Speedway. It had been set up perfectly for its "home track"—a fact that became clear to Hearne and Goux, who simply could not keep up.

Wilcox built a comfortable lead, cruised to victory, and was serenaded by the capacity crowd. His victory was bittersweet, however, for three men had died earlier in the race. On Lap 44, Arthur Thurman's car went too fast into a turn and rolled over him. On Lap 96, Louis LeCocq's Roamer exploded, killing him along with his riding mechanic, Robert Bandini. Both crashes were attributed to the new high speeds. After the race, Carl Fisher announced that engine specifications would be changed to limit speeds for the 1920 race.

Winner: Howdy Wilcox
Car: Peugeot
Speed: 88.1 mph
2. Eddie Hearne
3. Jules Goux
4. Albert Guyot
5. Tom Alley

1920

Heading into the 1920 Indy 500, there was concern that the new, less-powerful engines mandated by Carl Fisher might not hold up for a whole race. To make sure they would, qualifying runs were extended from one lap to four. And to prevent drivers from laying back and letting the leaders ruin their engines, the race now offered a $100 bonus for every lap led. Ralph DePalma grabbed the pole position with a top speed of 99.2 mph, and was anointed the race favorite. Since only 21 cars made the starting grid, his competition would be limited to a few familiar names, including Joe Boyer, Gaston Chevrolet, Rene Thomas, and Hardy Wilcox. Tommy Milton, a talented young driver who had nearly burned to death in a crash at a New Jersey race the previous summer, was back behind the wheel and also considered a legitimate challenger.

DePalma lost his lead on the pace lap, when his Ballot suffered a tire puncture. Boyer assumed command and kept his Frontenac in front for nearly half the race, with DePalma shadowing him. DePalma made his move on the 93rd lap, passing Boyer and establishing a solid lead. It looked like DePalma would become Indy's first two-time winner when, with 13 laps to go, his engine exploded into flames. His nephew and riding mechanic, Pete DePaolo, extinguished the fire and got the car started again, but first place was lost.

Now Chevrolet sped into first place. He was driving a Monroe built by his brothers, Arthur and Louis. Low on gas, he hoped to make it to the finish line. But on Lap 197 he heard his engine starting to sputter. Chevrolet glided into the pits, got just enough fuel for the final three laps, and pulled back onto the track before the second- and third-place cars driven by Thomas and Milton could catch up. He won with room to spare, piloting the first American-made car to win at Indy since 1912, and the first ever to complete all 500 miles without a tire change. Though the toast of the racing world, Chevrolet would not see his family's rise to automotive power, nor was he able to truly savor his fame. Seven months later young Gaston was killed while racing in California.

> **Winner: Gaston Chevrolet**
> Car: Monroe
> Speed: 88.2 mph
>   2. Rene Thomas
>   3. Tommy Milton
>   4. Jimmy Murphy
>   5. Ralph DePalma

1921

Gaston Chevrolet's death in December of 1920 seemed to dim enthusiasm for racing in 1921. This was illustrated by the fact that only 25 cars even bothered attempting to qualify for the Indy 500. Gaston's brothers, Arthur and Louis, decided to enter a car and they hired Tommy Milton to drive it. The purple and white Frontenac did not do well in qualifying, but the Chevrolets knew they had a good man behind the wheel. Pole position once again went to DePalma, and as usual he was one of the race favorites. Roscoe Sarles, Eddie Hearne, and Joe Boyer were also in the mix.

DePalma set a blistering pace from the opening lap, and after 100 laps the only thing he had to worry about was another bit

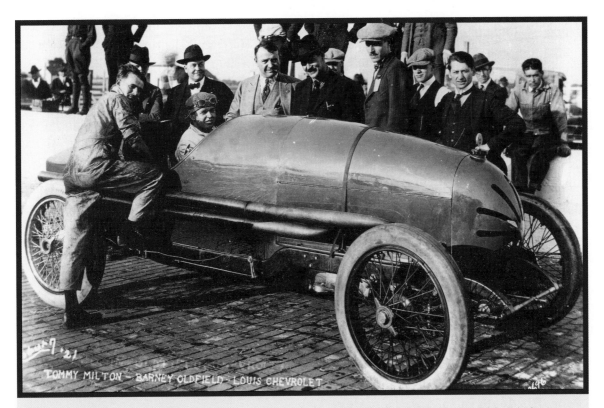

Tommy Milton proudly displays the winning car in the 1921 Indy 500. Living legend Barney Oldfield (with cigar) is standing beside him.

of bad luck. Twenty minutes later it happened—he lost a connecting rod and was through for the day. Milton, miles behind in second place, suddenly found himself in first. With no one else on the same lap, he drove straight and sure to give the Chevrolets their second straight Indy victory. It was a fitting tribute to their fallen brother.

Winner: Tommy Milton
Car: Frontenac
Speed: 89.6 mph
   2. Roscoe Sarles
   3. Percy Ford
   4. Eddie Miller
   5. Ora Haibe

1922

As the Chevrolet brothers rose to prominence during the postwar years at Indianapolis, so too did the Duesenberg brothers. Both families increased automobile sales for their companies when they did well. This was the reason factories put together racing teams—when a Frontenac won, people went out and bought Frontenacs from the Chevrolets; when "Duesies" dominated, the Duesenbergs saw sales skyrocket. At the 1922 race, 18 of the 27 qualifiers came from one of these two companies. The top qualifier was Jimmy Murphy, who topped 100 mph in a Duesenberg he dubbed the "Murphy Special." The car had brakes on all four wheels—a nov-

Jimmy Murphy, winner of the 1922 race. His death in 1924 was a major blow to racing.

94, and completed the 200 laps in record time. Hartz and Hearne made him sweat for a while, but Murphy managed to stay well ahead to take the checkered flag. Hearne's third-place Ballot was one of only two non-Duesies among the Top 10 finishers. It was quite a day for the Duesenbergs.

Winner: Jimmy Murphy
Car: Murphy
Speed: 94.5 mph
  2. Harry Hartz
  3. Eddie Hearne
  4. Ralph DePalma
  5. Ora Haibe

1923

The 1923 Indy 500 marked an important step for the event. New specifications brought engines in line with those used on the European racing circuit, which in turn brought a large contingent of European manufacturers and drivers to Indianapolis. Also, drivers were no longer required to ride with a mechanic, which really trained the spotlight on the wheel men. These changes, combined with the more powerful fuel that had been developed, sent qualifying speeds soaring. Despite rainy weather, five drivers topped the 100 mph mark, including Tommy Milton, who won the pole at 108.2 mph. Jimmy Murphy and Harry Hartz also turned in spectacular lap times, as did Cliff Durant, whose father's company had eight cars qualify. Another speedy qualifier was Ralph De-Palma, driving a Packard. His car was one of the few in this race that was not powered by an engine designed by automotive genius Harry Miller. Miller had built engines for

elty then, but soon to be the automotive standard. Murphy would have to prove to the 135,000 fans who jammed the Speed-way that he was the equal of top contenders Ralph DePalma, Jules Goux, Howdy Wilcox, and his old mentor, Tommy Milton.

When the green flag came down, Murphy blew everyone else off the track. Wilcox, Goux, and Milton pushed their cars to keep up, only to leave the race in the first hour with mechanical problems. That left Eddie Hearne's Ballot and a trio of factory Duesenbergs—driven by DePalma, Harry Hartz, and Ora Haibe—to chase Murphy down.

A year earlier, fans marveled at the 93 mph pace DePalma established before his car failed. This year Murphy averaged over

GREAT DRIVER: JIMMY MURPHY

Like so many children in San Francisco in 1906, Jimmy Murphy was orphaned during the earthquake that rocked the city. Unlike those other kids, Murphy had a plan. He was going to become a great race car driver. After being adopted by relatives in Southern California, he began hanging around race tracks and repair shops—learning all he could and waiting for someone to give him a chance. In 1916, at a race in Corona, driver Eddie O'Donnell needed a riding mechanic after his regular man fell ill. Murphy rode with O'Donnell, and they won the race.

After serving in the Air Service during World War I, Murphy came home and hooked up with Tommy Milton, the star of the Duesenberg racing team. Milton took Murphy under his wing and pushed for him to get his own car. By 1919, Murphy had won his first race. In 1920, he finished fourth—just behind Milton—in his first Indy start. At the end of the year Murphy stood second to Milton in the AAA point standings. The two parted ways when, while Milton was in the hospital, Murphy set a land speed record in a car built for Milton.

In 1921, Murphy traveled to France to enter the world's most prestigious racing event. No American had ever won a European Grand Prix in an American-built car, but Murphy ran bravely and outdistanced—by 15 minutes—the world's top drivers in his Duesy. He limped across the finish line on two flat tires, bloodied from road debris, in front of a stone-silent crowd. In a little over four hours, he had put American racing on the International map.

Murphy returned to a hero's welcome and proceeded to cement his reputation as the brightest star in American auto racing. He won the 1922 Indy 500 and was crowned national champion. In 1924, after he had already clinched the championship again, Murphy agreed to enter a dirt-track race in Syracuse, New York. While challenging for the lead, he skidded into the track's wooden railing. A large splinter broke off and pierced his heart.

fighter planes during the war, and was now developing motors that would dominate Indy for the rest of the decade.

Two crashes occurred in the early laps. Christian Lautenschlager, the only driver who opted for a riding mechanic, lost control of his car, but he and Jacob Krause walked away unhurt. A few minutes later, Tom Alley, driving in relief of Earl Cooper,

plowed his Durant through a wooden fence. Unfortunately, a group of teenagers was on the other side, watching the race through a knothole. Two were badly injured, and a third boy was killed. Meanwhile, the lead changed hands several times in the first half. For a while, it was Hardy Wilcox in his Miller-powered HCS who did the best driving, but clutch problems ended his day on

Lap 60. Milton then gained control, but had to be relieved when he developed blisters on his palms.

Milton chose Wilcox to drive for him, as the rules allowed. The Indiana native brought the crowd to its feet for a second time that day, leading the race for more than an hour while Milton received medical attention. When he climbed back into the cockpit, Hartz was right on his tail and his old friend and rival Murphy was not far behind—both driving yellow-and-red Durants. Milton's bandaged hands were killing him, but he grit his teeth and kept his foot on the gas the rest of the way to become Indy's first two-time champion. No one, however, was happier with the outcome than Miller. The top four cars all were powered by his engine.

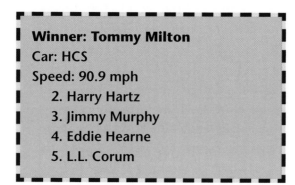

Winner: Tommy Milton
Car: HCS
Speed: 90.9 mph
   2. Harry Hartz
   3. Jimmy Murphy
   4. Eddie Hearne
   5. L.L. Corum

1924

Fans had much to talk about prior to the start of the 12th Indianapolis 500. Carl Fisher was no longer the head man at the Speedway, and his successor—co-founder James Allison—had already shaken things up. In previous years, only the Top 10 finishers received prize money. For this event a pool of $10,000 was created to be split among the rest of the drivers. Another item on the pre-race agenda was Duesenberg's supercharged

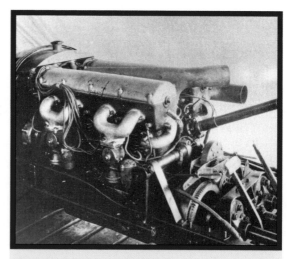

The elegant and efficient Duesenberg engine, which powered Indy winners in 1924, '25, and '27.

engine. This futuristic motor powered three cars in the race, driven by Joe Boyer, L.L. Corum, and Ernie Ansterburg. It was the first direct challenge to the supremacy of Harry Miller, who built 14 of the remaining 19 engines in the starting field.

The race itself started badly for the Duesenbergs. After Ansterburg wrecked and Boyer's engine started giving him trouble, their supercharged cars appeared to be out of the picture. This left the lead up for grabs and allowed Earl Cooper and Jimmy Murphy to give the fans something they had not seen in a while: a thrilling two-man duel. The see-saw battle between Cooper's Studebaker and Murphy's Miller lasted for more than 100 laps.

In the pits, Fred Duesenberg was growing angry and frustrated. Corum had the best car on the track, but was unable to catch the leaders. When he pitted on Lap 110, the car owner replaced him with Boyer, who had been fighting a balky supercharger all day. He told his top driver to chase down Murphy and Cooper. With just 22 laps to go, Boyer glided past the second-place Murphy, then overtook Cooper while he made his final pit stop. When the maroon car took the checkered flag, there were a lot of smiles at the Speedway. The Duesenbergs jumped for joy, Boyer took great satisfaction in making the most of this rare second chance, and Allison—the Brickyard's new boss—was pleased that his first race was one for the books.

Winner: L.L. Corum/Joe Boyer
Car: Duesenberg
Speed: 98.2 mph
2. Earl Cooper
3. Jimmy Murphy
4. Harry Hartz
5. Bennett Hill

1925

While racing fans spent the year wondering whether anything could top the thrills of the 1924 Indy 500, some important automotive breakthroughs were being made. Firestone introduced the "balloon" tire, which offered superior traction. And Harry Miller, determined to keep pace with the Duesenbergs, developed a supercharged engine of his own. He also debuted a front-wheel drive car, marking the first time this concept had been successfully applied to racing. The car was designed for Jimmy Murphy, who had been pondering retirement after winning his second U.S. driving championship in the summer of 1924. The thought of Murphy behind the wheel of a track-hugging, supercharged front-wheel drive vehicle was an exciting

one. Tragically, this potent combination never came to be, as Murphy was killed in a freak accident late in the 1924 season.

Fans watching qualifying at Indy the following spring could not help but think that it was a week the hard-charging Murphy really would have enjoyed. Speed records seemed to fall by the hour, as Earl Cooper, Peter DePaolo, Leon Duray, Harry Hartz, Ralph Hepburn, and Dave Lewis (driving Murphy's car) each broke Tommy Milton's old mark of 108.2 mph. Among the other luminaries driving supercharged cars were Ralph DePalma and Milton himself.

As soon as the green flag fell, DePaolo powered his Duesenberg to the front of the pack, passing the pole-sitter Duray. Lewis, driving a Miller Junior 8, was the only one able to keep pace. He caught up when DePaolo had to pit to get his blistered hands bandaged, but Lewis lost the lead after pitting on Lap 173. Too tired to continue, his relief driver Bennett Hill (whose car had

A mechanic marks up the Firestone Balloon tire, first introduced at Indy in 1925.

1925 Indy 500 "king" Peter DePaolo is flanked by the Duesenberg brothers, Augie and Fred.

race. Harry Miller did better than the Duesenbergs under the new modifications, as 17 of his engines made the starting field compared to only a couple of Duesies. Miller also had two front-wheel drive cars in the grid, driven by Earl Cooper and Dave Lewis. Cooper earned the pole with a qualifying speed of just under 112 mph. Among the 28 drivers who made the cut were plenty of familiar faces, including Peter DePaolo, Harry Hartz, and Leon Duray. Noticeably absent was Ralph DePalma, who had begun to move away from major events like the Indy 500.

One name that did not ring any bells was Frank Lockhart's. An unknown dirt-track driver from the West coast, Lockhart came to the Speedway as a relief man for owner-driver Peter Kreis. When Kreis fell ill prior to the race, Lockhart got to ride in his boss's white supercharged Miller. Starting from the 20th spot, Lockhart worked his

failed him more than 100 laps earlier) jumped behind the wheel and gave chase. Hill made up some ground, but DePaolo took the checkered flag less than a minute ahead of him. It was the smallest margin of victory to date, and the fastest race ever run, with average speeds topping 100 mph.

Winner: Peter DePaolo
Car: Duesenberg
Speed: 101.1 mph
   2. Dave Lewis
   3. Phil Shafer
   4. Harry Hartz
   5. Tommy Milton

1926

Fearful, once again, that increasing speeds would lead to disaster, Indy officials forced engine-makers to reduce power for the 1926

An up-close look at the workings of the Miller 1927 front-wheel-drive car. Many of today's automotive innovations trace their roots back to "The Brickyard."

way toward the front of the pack. No one paid much attention to his progress, as Lewis had a firm hold on the lead. But when Lewis's engine started to give him trouble, Lockhart moved past him. An hour later, with Lockhart still in the lead, the race was held up for an hour during a rainstorm.

When racing resumed, Hartz and De-Paolo caught Lockhart, but the Californian did not panic. After trailing Hartz for 15 minutes, he regained the lead. On Lap 160, with Lockhart still holding an edge, the pounding rains returned. With no break in the weather expected, the race was called off and Lockhart was crowned its champion.

Winner
Frank Lockhart-Miller Special

Frank Lockhart in his Miller Special. He came to Indy as an unknown relief driver and left as champion.

Winner: Frank Lockhart
Car: Miller
Speed: 95.9 mph
   2. Harry Hartz
   3. Cliff Woodbury
   4. Fred Comer
   5. Peter DePaolo

1927

Was Frank Lockhart a "flash in the pan?" The dirt-track specialist returned to the Brickyard in 1927 and erased any doubt about his talents when he piloted his rear-drive Miller to the astounding qualifying speed of 120.1 mph. With the defending champ starting in the pole position—and superstars Peter DePaolo, Leon Duray, Harry Hartz, Eddie Hearne, Dave Lewis, and Tommy Milton in the starting gird—fans settled in for an exciting race. Toward the back of the grid were a couple of Indiana natives named George Souders and

Wilbur Shaw. Souders, a local dirt-track star, was driving one of only three super-charged Duesenbergs to make the cut. Shaw, in a flashy gold Jynx, was wearing his trademark metal helmet. In his early days racing on dirt and wooden-board tracks, Shaw took a lot of teasing from the other drivers. But when he was thrown from his car, landed on his head, and walked away unhurt, those other drivers began to think that swapping leather headgear for metal wasn't such a bad idea.

Lockhart started the race where he had left off in qualifying. For 200 miles he was uncatchable—losing the lead only briefly when he made a long pit stop. Lockhart led for another 100 miles until, on Lap 120, he heard the sickening sound of a broken connector rod. This threw the race wide open, as Milton, Shaw, Hearne, and DePaolo jockeyed for position until DePaolo finally assumed command. As his pursuers faded, a new group moved up. Earl DeVore and Tony Gulotta, driving Millers, joined Babe Stapp and Souders in their Duesenbergs as they crept past the other drivers.

When DePaolo's yellow-and-black Miller began to misfire, Souders and the others surged past. In the final miles, Souders tore up the track. When he took the checkered flag, he was 12 minutes ahead of DeVore. The crowd mobbed Souders as he rolled into Victory Lane. Exhausted and dehydrated, all he cared about was getting something to drink...and letting his mother, at home in nearby Lafayette, know that he had won the race.

Winner: George Souders
Car: Duesenberg
Speed: 97.5 mph
    2. Earl DeVore
    3. Tony Gulotta
    4. Wilbur Shaw
    5. Dave Evans

1928

The Indianapolis Motor Speedway welcomed a new boss in 1928. Eddie Rickenbacker, the flying ace who competed in four Indys prior to World War I, bought the track from its original owners. Like everyone in racing, Rickenbacker was devastated when he heard the news that pre-race favorite Frank Lockhart had died while trying to set a new land-speed record in Florida. Some of the sadness was lifted during qualifying, when Leon Duray and Cliff Woodbury topped 120 mph. Fans could at least look forward to a fast race.

One person who was not happy in the

Eddie Rickenbacker, flanked by Tony Hulman and Wilbur Shaw, signs the papers transferring ownership of the Indianapolis Motor Speedway. Pop Myers, employed by the speedway since 1911, watches over Rickenbacker's shoulder.

days before the race was 23-year-old rookie Lou Meyer. The up-and-coming dirt-track star was promised a car by Augie Duesenberg, but when he received it, it was unassembled. A man named Sam offered to help Meyer put it together, and when they finished the job Duesenberg sold the car out from under them! Phil Shafer's Miller was for sale, but Meyer was in no position to buy much more than lunch. That is when Sam revealed his true identity: he was Alden Sampson II, a rich young sportsman whose family had countless millions. Sam bought the two-year-old rear-drive car and a dumstruck Meyer was back in the race.

Duray, in his Miller, took command early and held the lead at the midway point. But he pushed the car beyond its limits, and on Lap 133 it overheated. Jimmy Gleason, an exciting rookie, drove his Duesenberg into first place, with Tony Gulotta's Stutz close behind. These two battled for many laps until Gulotta began experiencing fuel problems. With no one close and just five laps to go, Gleason decided to get a splash of water for his radiator to prevent his car from overheating. A crew member stumbled and poured water over the entire engine, which sputtered, smoked, and died.

Meyer, who had been running a smooth, consistent race in his Miller, saw Gleason's car smoldering in the pits and realized that he was now in the lead. He also knew that Lou Moore was right behind him. Without batting an eye, the rookie slammed on the

gas and held off the second-place car, winning by just 44 seconds.

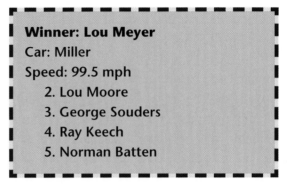

Winner: Lou Meyer
Car: Miller
Speed: 99.5 mph
   2. Lou Moore
   3. George Souders
   4. Ray Keech
   5. Norman Batten

1929

The racing world mourned the loss of two Indy 500 stars between the 1928 and 1929 events. Norman Batten and Earl DeVore were both vacationing on the SS Vestris cruise ship on November 12, 1928 when it sank in shark-infested waters. Batten, a driver noted for his bravery, was pulling survivors to safety when he was attacked by a shark. It is believed that DeVore met the same fate.

The 500 pushed on. Veteran Cliff Woodbury, was the lone qualifier to top 120 mph, and the first man out of the race. He wrecked on the third lap, but walked away. Bill Spence, driving for Augie Duesenberg was not as lucky. A few minutes after Woodbury's wreck, he lost control in a turn and was launched into the air when his car began to roll. He landed on his head and never regained consciousness.

Leon Duray grabbed the early lead but relinquished it after seven laps to Deacon Litz. Litz made what appeared to be a daring pass as he narrowly avoided a collision with Duray. In reality, Litz had reached for his hand-brake, only to find that it had fallen off earlier in the race—he had no

Eddie Rickenbacker, America's most beloved World War I flying ace. He took over at Indy in 1928.

choice but to swerve sharply out of trouble. Not one to look a gift horse in the mouth, Litz kept going and held the lead for 100 miles until a burned rod put him out of the race. At the race's midway point, the two Lou's—Meyer and Moore—were engaged in a spirited battle for first place. They see-sawed for 200 miles before the defending champion pulled into the pits for a quick oil change. When Meyer's car unexpectedly stalled, it took seven precious minutes to restart. By the time Meyer sped back onto the track, Ray Keech had caught and passed Moore, who was starting to have engine trouble of his own. Keech, driving a Simplex originally designed by the late Frank Lockhart, had finished fourth at Indy as a rookie in 1928. Those who had questioned his experience and driving skill now had their answer. Keech maintained his six-minute advantage right to the finish line. Incredibly, the bizarre string of racing fatalities continued when, two weeks later, Keech, the newly crowned Indy 500 champ perished during a race in Pennsylvania.

Winner: Ray Keech
Car: Simplex
Speed: 97.6
  2. Lou Meyer
  3. Jimmy Gleason
  4. Carl Marchese
  5. Freddy Winnai

1930

The Great Depression, which began when the stock market crashed in the fall of 1929, hit the automotive industry extremely hard. Even the strongest car companies watched helplessly as sales plummeted and the value of their stock hit rock bottom. The effect on auto racing was devastating, too. Although Indy cars were not plastered with decals as they are today, they were essentially "rolling advertisements" for the auto, tire, and engine companies. If no one was buying cars, there was no reason to invest in advertising. With no advertisers to sponsor drivers, they could barely afford to compete. By May, it was clear that the 500 would have to make some drastic changes.

Given that the 1930 entries would be older cars that had been racing in 1928 and 1929, it seemed, to Eddie Rickenbacker, like a good idea to bring back the riding mechanic. He could hold things together on the fly, thus limiting the amount of time spent in the pits. Rickenbacker also lowered the qualifying speed, to ensure that enough cars actually made the starting grid. The changes prompted critics to refer to the 1930 race as the "Junkyard Formula." Although Billy Arnold claimed the pole position, most believed that meteoric Lou Meyer, driving a car built by his millionaire friend Alden Sampson II, was the race favorite.

As anticipated, the race was a sloppy one from the start. Chet Gardner spun out in his Buckeye and never completed his first trip around the track. A multi-car pile up on Lap 23 knocked seven drivers out of action. Minutes later, Cy Marshall crashed into the wall and watched as his brother Paul—who was serving as riding mechanic—was pitched to his death.

In between wrecks, Arnold passed Meyer and took the lead. Amazingly, he managed to hold it the rest of the way and was never seriously challenged. Arnold finished well ahead of the pack, and earned a record $50,300 for his surprising perfor-

Two men ride in each car at the start of the 1930 Indy 500. Racing teams, financially strapped by the Great Depression, returned to the day of the riding mechanic to reduce maintenance costs.

mance. The most interesting moment of the day came courtesy of Chet Miller. Driving on a Ford Model T chassis, he pulled into the pits after breaking a spring. When his crew informed him they had not brought a replacement, Miller improvised. He sprinted to the parking lot, spotted a Model T, and "borrowed" the part he needed. Minutes later he was back in the race, and finished 13th!

Winner: Billy Arnold
Car: Miller-Hartz
Speed: 100.4 mph
   2. Shorty Cantlon
   3. Louis Schneider
   4. Lou Meyer
   5. Bill Cummings

1931

As the Depression deepened, so too did the desperate position in which auto racing found itself. Nothing had improved since 1930, so the same rules were in effect for the 1931 Indy 500. A record 70 cars attempted to make the expanded starting field of 40, including some "stock" cars made by Chrysler, Buick, and Ford. Among the more well known qualifiers were Shorty Cantlon, Jimmy Gleason, Tony Gulotta, Lou Meyer, Lou Schneider, Wilbur Shaw, Russ Snowberger, and defending champion Billy Arnold.

Rain delayed the start for two hours, but as soon as the green flag came down, Arnold began setting a fast pace and held the lead from Lap 7 until he crashed on Lap 162. Twenty-one cars were out of the race

Lou Schneider poses with mechanic Jigger Johnson. After finishing third in 1930, Schneider took the checkered flag in 1931.

by this time, but Arnold's wreck was by far the most serious. The defending champion fractured his pelvis when his gray and blue Miller-Hartz spun into the wall, and his mechanic broke his shoulder. The steering wheel flew completely out of the race course onto Georgetown Road, where it struck and killed an 11-year-old boy. Schneider and Fred Frame moved into the lead, with Schneider finally gaining an advantage with 34 laps left. He won the race by a mere 43 seconds.

Winner: Lou Schneider
Car: Bowes Seal-Fast Special
Speed: 96.6 mph
  2. Fred Frame
  3. Ralph Hepburn
  4. Myron Stevens
  5. Russ Snowberger

1932

The Great Depression was at its low point and, once again, the Indy 500 featured a starting grid made up of the flotsam and jetsam of the economically crippled automotive industry. Forty cars, ranging from a four-cylinder Lion Head Special driven by Howdy Wilcox II (no relation to the 1919 race-winner) to an ear-splitting, 16-cylinder Miller piloted by Lou Meyer, roared away when the green flag came down. The smart money was on Lou Moore, who turned in a 117 mph qualifying time. But Billy Arnold, Lou Schneider, and Fred Frame all had fast cars and good track records at the Speedway.

Moore and Arnold led early, setting a record pace. Arnold went out of the race on Lap 59, in a weird replay of his 1931 wreck. He and his mechanic were thrown over the wall after swerving to avoid another car. Arnold, who retired after the race, broke his shoulder and Spider Matlock fractured his pelvis—the exact opposite of the injuries they had suffered 12 months earlier!

Bob Carey, a rookie driving a car owned by Lou Meyer, took the lead briefly before spinning out. Next came a group including Frame, Wilcox, Cliff Bergere and Russ Snowberger. The lead pack finally thinned out with about 50 laps to go. The veteran Frame established himself as the man to beat, with Wilcox chasing. Frame took the checkered flag, a mile in front of the second-place car.

> **Winner: Fred Frame**
> **Car: Miller-Hartz**
> **Speed: 104.1 mph**
>   2. Howdy Wilcox II
>   3. Cliff Bergere
>   4. Bob Carey
>   5. Russ Snowberger

1933

Although the economy was starting to reawaken, to the auto racing world there seemed no end in sight to the bad times plaguing the United States. During the months leading up to the 1933 race, it was announced that prize money would be cut by almost half. This, in combination with a threatened driver's strike, nearly shut down the Indy 500 for the first time since World War I. The dispute was settled in time for qualifying, which was staged in a 10-lap format for the first time. Bill Cummings took the pole with a speed of 118.5 mph. Howdy Wilcox II, a race favorite who turned in a speed of 117.6 mph, was disqualified on the eve of the race when it was

learned he had diabetes. When his fellow drivers protested, Eddie Rickenbacker struck a compromise and allowed Wilcox's car (driven by Mauri Rose) to enter the race.

Cummings and defending champion Fred Frame jockeyed for the lead during the first 90 minutes, until Cummings retired with a broken valve. Frame led the pack for another 50 laps before his engine overheated. Babe Stapp surged into the lead, but he miscalculated his fuel use and ran out of gas on Lap 157.

Lou Meyer, the 1928 winner, recognized an opportunity when he saw one. He had been running smoothly just off the lead, and now he took command. He built an advantage over Wilbur Shaw and maintained it to become the second two-time winner. His speed of 104.2 mph broke the record set by Frame the previous year. But what history remembers best about this finish is that, when Meyer pulled into Victory Lane, he glugged down a bottle of milk—a tradition for the Indy 500 champion to this day.

> **Winner: Lou Meyer**
> **Car: Tydol**
> **Speed: 104.2 mph**
>   2. Wilbur Shaw
>   3. Lou Moore
>   4. Chet Gardner
>   5. Stubby Stubblefield

1934

Safety was on the minds of Indy officials in 1934. Three men had died in two accidents during the 1933 race, and high speed was blamed in both cases. To reduce speed and relieve congestion, the field was cut from 42 to 33 cars, and teams were limited to 45 gallons of gas for the entire race. Although this was more than enough to complete the 200 laps, it forced drivers to pace themselves and take fewer risks. Lou Meyer was favored to repeat his 1933 victory, but there would be several serious challengers. Kelly Petillo claimed the pole at 119.3 mph, while Frank Brisko, Bill Cummings, Wilbur Shaw, and Mauri Rose all had excellent cars.

Petillo led for six laps before having to make an unexpected pit stop. Brisko, who began the day third on the starting grid, took the lead and held it for 69 laps. When he faded, Cummings and Rose began a 200-mile duel for first place. For the "engine men" in the stands this was an exciting development, for it pitted a rear-drive Miller (Rose) against a front-drive Miller (Cummings). Meyer, who hoped these two would burn each other out, never got a chance to make his move. Just before the midway point, his oil tank sprung a leak, which finished him. On the 175th lap, Cummings finally put some distance between himself and Rose. Although the race remained close, Cummings piloted his red-white-and-blue Boyle Products Special to victory at record speed, with Rose less than a half-minute behind.

Despite hard times—which crippled sports like pro football and basketball—the Indy 500 continued to grow in stature. Attendance for the 1934 race topped 140,000. If you were into racing, the Indianapolis Motor Speedway was the place to be seen each May. That was even true for John Dillinger, the "Most Wanted" man in America. The famed bank robber was in the stands for the race, and even signed autographs!

> **Winner: Bill Cummings**
> **Car: Boyle Products Special**
> **Speed: 104.9 mph**
> 2. Mauri Rose
> 3. Lou Moore
> 4. Deacon Litz
> 5. Joe Russo

1935

The 1935 Indy 500 marked the beginning of a long and successful run for the Offenhauser engine, a powerful offshoot of a motor designed by Harry Miller for the boating industry. The "Offy" would be propelling drivers to victory at the Brickyard right through the 1970s, but during qualifying in '35 they did not exactly take Indy by storm. Wilbur Shaw and Kelly Petillo had the new engines, and they placed 20th and 22nd—far behind pole winner Rex Mays, who turned in a speed of 120.7 mph. Far more noticeable to the average fan were some additional safety regulations, including mandatory crash helmets and a system of lights positioned at strategic points, which let drivers know if they could expect trouble ahead. A yellow light required everyone to slow to 75 mph.

Petillo, driving a red-and-cream Wetteroth dubbed the Gilmore Speedway Special, had the fastest car in the race. His best qualifying time had been thrown out on a technicality, but the Californian streaked to the front of the pack once the green flag dropped. There he encountered Mays. The two staged an intense battle until Lap 60, when Mays pulled into the pits. He caught up quickly and regained the lead, but on the 123rd lap a bad spring shackle put him out of the race.

Petillo had little time to enjoy his good fortune, for soon Shaw's Offy-powered front-wheel-drive Pirrung roared past him. Petillo waited for Shaw to pit and pulled into first place. This time Petillo's luck held; when Shaw returned to the track, a light rain was falling and speeds were reduced for 14 laps. Shaw never had a chance to make up ground, and Petillo streaked across the finish line with an average speed of 106.2 mph, the fourth year in a row the track record had fallen. Unfortunately, good luck did not smile on Clay Weatherly and Stubby Stubblefield. Both died in crashes—one of which also took the life of Stubblefield's mechanic, Leo Whittaker.

Winner: Kelly Petillo
Car: Gilmore Speedway Special
Speed: 106.2 mph
   2. Wilbur Shaw
   3. Bill Cummings
   4. Floyd Roberts
   5. Ralph Hepburn

1936

Lou Meyer had been the last man on the track when the 1935 Indy 500 ended. Although simply making it through the whole race is quite an accomplishment, Meyer ached to return to Victory Lane. Imagine how disappointed he was after qualifying a lowly 28th for the 1936 race. Rex Mays, Babe Stapp, Chet Miller, and Doc MacKenzie, meanwhile, looked like the men to beat when the day began. They had turned in the top four times at the revamped Brickyard, which now featured outer walls designed to keep cars from flying off the track.

Lou Meyer accepts the Borg-Warner Trophy for winning the 1936 Indy 500.

A total of 10 cars in the starting grid had Offy engines, including Wilbur Shaw's. He moved into the lead when Mays pitted with throttle problems, and held the top spot for more than 150 miles. On Lap 83, Shaw noticed his hood was rattling and left the track for a quick repair. Fifteen minutes later he was still in the pits, and at that point out of contention. From then on, the old reliable Miller engines ruled the day.

Meyer, who had moved up slowly from the rear, eased into first place. He refueled on Lap 131, at which point Ted Horn gained the lead. When Horn pitted, Meyer regained control. He maintained his advantage in his Miller-powered Ring Free Special, taking the checkered flag and shattering the year-old course record. Meyer, a clever and talented driver, became Indy's first three-time winner. He was also the first man to receive the now-familiar silver Borg-Warner trophy. The great Tommy Milton, who drove the Packard pace car to start the race, suggested that Meyer get to drive it home, marking the beginning of another Brickyard tradition.

> **Winner: Lou Meyer**
> Car: Ring Free Special
> Speed: 109.1 mph
> 2. Ted Horn
> 3. Doc MacKenzie
> 4. Mauri Rose
> 5. Chet Miller

1937

Eddie Rickenbacker continued his campaign to make Indy safer, outlawing the "special brew" fuels used by different teams

The Indy 500 pace car is usually the "cream of the crop" in American auto manufacturing. This gleaming Packard 120 led the field for the opening lap of the 1936 race.

and requiring everyone to use the same kind of gas. The track boss also began to replace the Brickyard's brick surface with smooth asphalt. Although the race itself was accident-free, a fiery practice crash took the life of Otto Rhode, the crew chief for Champion Spark Plugs. A fireman also perished in the pit row blaze.

The three top drivers—Bill Cummings, Wilbur Shaw, and Herb Ardinger—each broke the course qualifying record in Offy-powered vehicles. But it was Jimmy Snyder who attempted to set the early clip. He careened around the track at a record-setting pace before his transmission finally blew. Shaw took charge, driving a car he had built himself, with Cummings and Ralph Hepburn behind him.

With no one able to mount a strong challenge, Shaw looked good with 20 laps to go. As he neared the finish line, however, his oil gauge began to drop. Shaw throttled back to preserve his engine, which gave Hepburn an opening. Going into the last lap, Hepburn was poised to overtake the leader. Realizing he had no choice, Shaw slammed on the accelerator and held his breath. His Offy held up, but his lead continued to evaporate. With the crowd on its feet and screaming wildly, Shaw crossed the line just two seconds in front of the fast-closing Hepburn.

> **Winner: Wilbur Shaw**
> Car: Shaw-Gilmore
> Speed: 113.6 mph
> 2. Ralph Hepburn
> 3. Ted Horn
> 4. Lou Meyer
> 5. Cliff Bergere

GREAT DRIVER: WILBUR SHAW

During the 1920s, when American racing enjoyed an incredible surge in popularity, Wilbur Shaw was the terror of the Midwest. He could win in any car on any surface, and specialized in board-track events. In 1923, Shaw crashed and fractured his skull. When doctors told him he would probably die if he crunched his cranium again, he fashioned a metal crash helmet and got right back behind the wheel.

Other drivers laughed when they saw him—they were still wearing leather helmets—which were quite dashing but offered little protection in high-speed accidents. Shortly thereafter, Shaw was thrown from his car in a violent crash, and landed on his head. Shaken but still alive, he walked away, and soon metal helmets became mandatory.

By the mid-1930s, Shaw had worked his way into the upper tier of American racing. In 1930, he finished 24th in his first Indy 500 start, and won the race seven years later. Shaw then accepted an offer to race in Europe, where he drove a Maserati for the first time. When war broke out, he returned to the U.S. and began racing his Maserati in American events.

Shaw won back-to-back 500s in 1939 and 1940—becoming the first to do so—and was in the lead in 1941 when a broken wheel hub sent him spinning out of control. The injuries he suffered in this crash ended his racing career, but after the war he convinced Tony Hulman to buy the track and stayed on as president and general manager until his death in a plane crash in 1954.

Although he never thought of himself as a pioneer, Shaw turned out to be a pivotal figure in American racing. His introduction of the first piece of safety equipment used in racing and his campaign to save the Indianapolis Motor Speedway from the wrecking ball twice altered the course of the sport.

1938

The Indianapolis 500 continued to move bravely into the modern era in 1938. For the first time during the 1930s, mechanics were back in the pits, not in the passenger seats. Also, new engine standards were adopted to keep pace with changes on the European Grand Prix circuit. And an "electric eye" was introduced to more precisely measure speeds and lap times. The race figured to be a fast one. Although the economy was still suffering, there was finally enough money around the automotive industry to develop powerful racing engines. Qualifying speeds soared into the mid-120s, with Floyd Roberts and Ronney Householder topping 125 mph.

Rex Mays, driving a sleek new supercharged Alfa Romeo, took control early. After 45 laps, he gave way to Jimmy Snyder, who did a magnificent job holding off Roberts and Householder. With 50 laps to go, Snyder's Sparks engine could no longer handle the strain and he was forced to retire. Moments later Householder's Sparks engine suffered the same fate. That left Roberts with a four-lap lead over second-place Wilbur Shaw, and he cruised to an easy victory.

> **Winner: Floyd Roberts**
> Car: Burd Piston Ring Special
> Speed: 117.2 mph
>   2. Wilbur Shaw
>   3. Chet Miller
>   4. Ted Horn
>   5. Chet Gardner

1939

With all of the safety measures introduced at Indy during the 1930s, fans could be excused for thinking the 500 might one day become a "safe" race. They had to think again after 1939. Qualifying came off without any crack-ups, as Jimmy Snyder grabbed the pole with a speed over 130 mph. Among the favorites were Lou Meyer, Wilbur Shaw, Ted Horn, and defending champion Floyd Roberts, all of whom turned in practice laps at 128 mph or more.

Snyder assumed command of the race until the first pit stop, when Shaw nudged in front of Meyer to take the lead. Snyder pulled back into first place when Shaw and Meyer pitted. For the first half of the race, this three-way battle continued. On Lap 107 the race turned ugly when, behind the leaders, several cars spun out and and smashed into one another. Chet Miller, the 1938 third-place finisher, tried to dodge through the traffic but slammed into the pile and was se-

riously hurt. Seconds later, Floyd Roberts attempted to swerve around the chaos but struck another car which had just spun free. Roberts, one of the sport's most popular drivers, broke his neck in the accident and died.

When order was finally restored, Meyer, Shaw, and Snyder were still in front. Shaw's maroon "Boyle Special" Maserati passed Meyer with 40 miles to go, but could not shake him. As he prepared to make a run at his fourth Indy win, Meyer had a tire explode and came within inches of creasing the wall. He repaired the tire and got back on the track, only to smash into the inside rail less than three laps short of the finish line. Meanwhile, Shaw held off Snyder to win his second Indy 500. It marked the first time in two decades a foreign car had prevailed at the Brickyard. After the race, Meyer decided to retire; he did not want to go out the way Roberts and so many of his friends had.

> **Winner: Wilbur Shaw**
> Car: Boyle Special
> Speed: 115.0 mph
>   2. Jimmy Snyder
>   3. Cliff Bergere
>   4. Ted Horn
>   5. Babe Stapp

1940

With Lou Meyer gone, Wilbur Shaw was now the undisputed king of American racing. He would test his skill at Indy on the newly resurfaced track, which now showed brick only on a section of the front straightaway. Shaw's chief rival figured to be Rex Mays, along with Mauri Rose, Ted Horn, and Mel Hansen—all of whom qualified in the top five. The race began under a shroud of sadness, as everyone mourned the death of George Bailey. The popular driver had crashed in practice. His car owner, the great Harry Miller, had seen enough death in one lifetime, and decided he would no longer sponsor cars at Indy.

Mays, Shaw, and Rose opened up a quick lead on the rest, but all eyes were on Raul Riganti. The daring Argentinian's Maserati was weaving toward the front of the pack at breakneck speed. No one was surprised when his car hit the wall and rolled on the 25th lap. How he walked away from the horrific crash is still a mystery.

Mays led for most of the early going but Shaw made his move and opened up a one-lap lead. Dark clouds began gathering over the track, and by the 150th lap a soft rain had turned into a downpour. The rest of the race was run under caution, which meant Mays and Rose never had a chance to catch up. With this ho-hum victory, Shaw became the first back-to-back Indy champion and matched Meyer's feat of three career victories.

Winner: Wilbur Shaw
Car: Boyle Special
Speed:114.3 mph
  2. Rex Mays
  3. Mauri Rose
  4. Ted Horn
  5. Joel Thorne

1941

Fans at the 1941 Indy 500 had a funny feeling that this would be the last race they would be watching at the Brickyard for a while. War was raging in Europe again, and it seemed only a matter of time before America joined the Allied cause against the Axis powers of Germany, Italy, and Japan. That would mean no racing for the duration, much as it had been during the last global conflict. Only 42 cars attempted to qualify for the starting grid, only 33 cars made it, and—thanks to a practice crash and a fire in the garage area—only 31 were there on race day. Mauri Rose held the pole position, while Rex Mays and Wilbur Shaw also turned in swift qualifying times.

Rose started well, and was leading the race after 39 laps. On Lap 40, however, he encountered spark plug problems and had to take his Maserati out of the race. That left owner Lou Moore with just one other car, a Wetteroth sponsored by Noc-Out Hose Clamps. The car was driven by Floyd Davis. He was a good dirt-track man but not remotely in Rose's class as an Indy driver. Davis had started the day in 17th place, and despite the fact that four cars in front of him had dropped out, he was running 14th (in effect, he had gone back one place). After 71 laps, Moore decided to pull Davis from the cockpit and replace him with Rose.

Davis was furious when Rose sped off in the Noc-Out Special, but he watched in awe with everyone else as his teammate skillfully picked his way toward the front of the pack. Meanwhile, Shaw was humming right along. His car had narrowly escaped damage in the pre-race blaze, thanks to quick work by firefighters. But when they hosed down his car, they inadvertently washed away a chalk marking on one of his wheels indicating it needed to be replaced. In the ensuing confusion, no one remembered.

Indy legend Mauri Rose (l.) and dirt-track journeyman Floyd Davis (r.) share the post-race glory in 1941.

When the wheel collapsed on Lap 152, Shaw knew instantly what had happened. As he cursed his luck, Cliff Bergere zoomed into the lead. He held this spot for just 10 laps, until Rose completed his amazing comeback and grabbed first place. Rose held Mays off for the final 25 miles to earn a shared victory with the now-ecstatic Davis, who was the last man anyone every expected to be sipping milk in Victory Lane.

Winner: Floyd Davis/Mauri Rose
Car: Noc-Out Hose Clamp Special
Speed: 115.1 mph
  2. Rex Mays
  3. Ted Horn
  4. Ralph Hepburn
  5. Cliff Bergere

CHAPTER 3

THE GOLDEN YEARS

1946

The United States did indeed enter the war, and the Indy 500 was cancelled from 1942 through 1945. The Indianapolis Motor Speedway was pressed into service as a testing ground for tires during World War II, but the military did little to provide for its upkeep. Wilbur Shaw, who retired after the 1941 race, was appalled at the track's condition when he visited for a tire test. Soon after the war ended, he persuaded a local businessman named Tony Hulman to buy the Speedway from Eddie Rickenbacker, whose interest had now turned to his new company, Eastern Airlines. Hulman paid Rickenbacker $750,000, then appointed Shaw as track president and general manager.

Shaw worked feverishly to get the dilapidated track in shape in time for the 1946 Indy 500. He offered the then-staggering sum of $115,000 in prize money, which lured nearly five dozen entries. It was "back to the future" time during qualifying, as fans watched 58 cars—some of which were leftover from the 1930s!—vie for a spot in the 33-car starting field. Among the familiar faces were Rex Mays, Mauri Rose, Ralph

Hepburn, Ted Horn, and Cliff Bergere, who won the pole position in his Noc-Out Special. Fans were disappointed when the famous European champion, Rudolph Caracciola, arrived without his Mercedes (it was impounded by customs agents), and then again when he crashed attempting to qualify in an unfamiliar car.

Mays and Rose tried to set a fast pace early in the race, but were both out of action within 45 minutes—Mays with a damaged engine manifold and Rose, after a crash. Hepburn led for a while, but his motor gave out mid-race. That left the door open for George Robson, a driver who had just been getting his feet wet at Indy before the war came. He maneuvered his blue-and-white Adams, entered by Thorne Engineering, into first place. And there he remained. Robson's lone challenger was rookie Jimmy Jackson, behind the wheel of an old Miller he had rebuilt and modified himself. This unlikely duo tore up the track while the more famous drivers fell one-by-one to mechanical problems. When Robson took the checkered flag, only eight others were still running.

Winner: George Robson
Car: Adams
Speed: 114.8 mph
   2. Jimmy Jackson
   3. Ted Horn
   4. Emil Andres
   5. Joie Chitwood

1947

Race car drivers are supposed to have excellent timing. This was not the case in 1947, when the newly formed American Society of Professional Auto Racing (ASPAR) threatened to boycott the Indy 500 unless Tony Hulman shared more of the profits with them. Wilbur Shaw promised to raise the prize money by more than $15,000, but by the time ASPAR accepted this offer, it was too late for many racing teams to get their cars ready for qualifying. The result was that the richest race in Indy history only had 30 qualifiers. That was fine with Ted Horn. The Indy veteran was one of only three drivers to top 125 mph, and was thus installed as one of the race favorites along with Mauri Rose, Cliff Bergere, and rookie Bill Holland.

Holland pushed his Blue Crown Spark Plug Special to an early lead, which he held for nearly 40 laps before losing control of his car for just an instant. In that instant, Bergere streaked past him. Shorty Cantlon spun out trying to avoid Holland and slammed into the wall. Cantlon hit the concrete hard, and never regained consciousness. Bergere kept the top spot until a burned piston ended his day on the 64th lap.

Holland regained the lead, but Rose, also driving a Blue Crown for team owner Lou Moore, was closing fast. No one else was near these two, so Moore motioned both drivers into the pits for a final refueling with 8 laps to go. Holland swerved down into pit row, got a quick splash of gas, and then reentered the track. He finished the final laps assuming he was the leader. But

Bill Holland and crew. After two second-place finishes, Holland won the 1949 race.

Rose never pitted! Disobeying Moore's orders, the crafty veteran had decided to stay on the track—and was now a half-minute ahead of his unsuspecting rookie teammate. Holland was shocked when he crossed the finish line to find that the checkered flag had already been dropped.

> **Winner: Mauri Rose**
> **Car: Blue Crown Spark Plug Special**
> **Speed: 116.3 mph**
> 2. Bill Holland
> 3. Ted Horn
> 4. Herb Ardinger
> 5. Jimmy Jackson

1948

The controversial one-two finish of Mauri Rose and Bill Holland in 1947 made them co-favorites for the 1948 Indy 500. But in the days before the race, the talk of the track was the Novi V-8 engine. It was incredibly powerful, and many drivers —including veterans Cliff Bergere and Chet Miller—refused to go near it. Bergere's replacement, Ralph Hepburn, took his car out in practice and lost control on the track's third turn. He hit the wall with tremendous force, and died on impact. Besides Rose and Holland, fans were also watching Rex Mays, who won his record fourth pole, and Billy DeVore, who was driving a outlandish six-wheel Kurtis built by Pat Clancy.

Mays started fast as always, leading for 36 laps before being overtaken. A series of challengers took and then lost the lead until the trio of Holland, Rose, and Ted Horn established itself in front of the pack. Horn, the 1947 national driving champ, seemed to

be in command in his Maserati, which had been outfitted by renowned innovator Cotton Henning.

All was not as it appeared, however. The two feared their car might falter down the stretch, because prior to the race, they had found evidence of sabotage; someone had poured sand into the engine. They were able to flush out all but a few granules, but those had the potential to cause excessive wear as the race wore on. Horn's heart sank when he saw his oil pressure drop, and he had no choice but to ease up and let Lou Moore's drivers streak past him. This time, there would be no phantom pit stops. Both men floored it all the way to the finish, with Rose winning fair and square this time. He joined Wilbur Shaw and Louis Meyer as the only three-time Indy winners.

> **Winner: Mauri Rose**
> **Car: Blue Crown Spark Plug Special**
> **Speed: 119.8 mph**
> 2. Bill Holland
> 3. Duke Nalon
> 4. Ted Horn
> 5. Mack Hellings

1949

Television was still in its infancy in 1949, but there were enough televisions in Indiana—and enough racing fans—for local station WFMB to televise the race for the first time. Despite the fact that Duke Nalon won the pole position, everyone watching the race was hoping for the same thing: another showdown between teammates Mauri Rose and Bill Holland.

More than 175,000 people filled the

stands at the Brickyard as Nalon set a record pace in the early going. He had finished a lucky third a year earlier using the dangerous Novi engine, but this year his luck ran out on lap 24, when he snapped an axle, crashed, and was engulfed in a fireball. Though badly burned, Nalon survived. Rex Mays, also driving a Novi Mobil, took the lead, but engine problems forced him out after 47 laps. (It would be the popular driver's final appearance at Indy; six months later he was killed racing in California). Holland took the lead and drove like he meant to keep it. By the midway point of the race, the only one with a chance to catch him was Rose. This was the race everyone had been hoping for!

In a replay of the 1947 drama, Moore begged his drivers to ease up. A one-two finish was practically guaranteed. As he had two years earlier, Holland obeyed his boss's instructions. And once again, Rose did not. Rose needed only to complete nine laps for his third straight victory, but this time his hard driving caught up with him. He busted a magneto strap and had to pull off the course for repairs. Holland must have been grinning when he passed Rose in the pits. No longer second-best, he crossed the finish line miles ahead of rookie, Johnnie Parsons. As Holland glided into Victory Lane, he looked around for Lou Moore, who was nowhere to be found. He was too busy firing Rose.

> **Winner: Bill Holland**
> **Car: Blue Crown Spark Plug Special**
> **Speed: 121.3 mph**
>   2. Johnnie Parsons
>   3. George Connor
>   4. Myron Fohr
>   5. Joie Chitwood

1950

The racing world could barely wait for "round four" of the heavyweight battle between Bill Holland and Mauri Rose. Adding to the drama in 1950 was the fact that these two drivers were now on different teams. Holland was still racing for Lou Moore, while Rose had signed with owner Howard Keck. Newcomer Walt Faulkner, a midget-car champion, put his name in the hat by winning the pole, and Johnnie Parsons was also in the mix after finishing second the year before. Still, it was the Holland-Rose rivalry that sent attendance soaring.

Rose, driving an Offenhauser from the number-three position, led for nine laps until Parsons whizzed past him. Parsons's crew had discovered a minute crack in his engine that morning and concluded that he would be unable to complete more than a few dozen laps. So he decided to drive as hard as he could and pick up a few bonus dollars for each lap he led before his motor conked out. Behind Parsons, Rose and Holland were at it again. The former teammates battled each other with ferocity and cunning; sometimes it seemed as if no one else was on the track.

As the midway point came and went, strange things started happening. The normally cautious Holland missed the entrance to the pit area, costing him valuable time. Rose, meanwhile, watched in dismay as his car caught fire during a routine pit stop. Strangest of all was the fact that Parsons kept zooming around the track, with no sign that his engine was about to blow. Holland and Rose soon realized that they had better start driving for first place instead of second, and they closed to within a few hundred yards of Parsons. Just then the skies opened up and the rains came. The track quickly became too treacherous, and the race was called off after just 138 laps. A drenched and smiling Parsons pulled his bright yellow Kurtis into Victory Lane knowing he'd out-pointed the sport's two biggest heavyweights.

> **Winner: Johnnie Parsons**
> **Car: Wynn's Friction Proof Special**
> **Speed: 124.0 mph**
>   **2. Bill Holland**
>   **3. Mauri Rose**
>   **4. Cecil Green**
>   **5. Joie Chitwood**

1951

After four years of Rose vs. Holland, the focus of the Indy 500 began to turn to some of the sport's new drivers. Making their first Indy starts were the promising trio of Rodger Ward, Mike Nazaruk, and Bill Vukovich. Lee Wallard, who had been turning in respectable performances at Indy since 1948, qualified second. The top qualifier was Duke Nalon, while Jack McGrath, Duane Carter, and Mauri Rose also had hot cars.

As soon as the green flag dropped, Wallard and McGrath strained to grab the lead. Nalon dropped back with ignition trouble, while the rookies Vukovich and Ward went out of the race with oil-related problems. By the halfway point, 16 of the 33 cars had fallen to mechanical difficulties. This made it easy for Wallard and McGrath to stay out in front.

Rose, who had designs on his fourth Indy win, was nearly killed when one of his

wheels collapsed on the 127th lap. His car went tumbling into the infield. Unhurt but badly shaken, he retired after the race. By this time, Wallard had put some distance between himself and McGrath, but his car was failing, too. His brakes were nearly gone when he screamed across the finish line, well ahead of the rookie Nazaruk. A few weeks later, Wallard suffered terrible burns during a race in California. Although he returned to racing, he was never able to sweat normally again so that his body could cool down. This prevented him from entering long, hot races like the Indy 500, which required great stamina.

> **Winner: Lee Wallard**
> **Car: Belanger Special**
> **Speed: 126.2 mph**
>   **2. Mike Nazaruk**
>   **3. Jack McGrath**
>   **4. Andy Linden**
>   **5. Bob Ball**

1952

The buzz at Indy in 1952 revolved around three very different entries. At one end of the spectrum was the Cummins Diesel Special, a car driven by Fred Agabashian and built by the Cummins Corporation at a reported cost of $500,000—a staggering amount at the time. At the other end of the spectrum was the number-seven qualifier, Troy Ruttman. The 22-year-old Californian looked like a baby compared to some of the Indy veterans. With three Indy starts already under his belt, he was driving a modest little dirt-track Kuzma owned by Texan J.C. Agajanian, with a price tag representing a mere fraction of that of the Cummins car's. The third intriguing entry was a Ferrari driven by Italian superstar Alberto Ascari.

Ninety minutes into the race, two of these three vehicles were done for the day—the high-profile Cummins and the sleek, sexy Ferrari! Meanwhile, Ruttman was cruising right along, right behind fellow Californian Bill Vukovich, who held the lead for much of the afternoon. With just 10 laps to go, the steering on Vukovich's Fuel Injection Special gave out and he skidded into the wall. With no pursuers in sight, Ruttman calmly drove the last 25 miles to become the youngest winner in race history.

mina. No fewer than 10 drivers had to be relieved during the race. One, Carl Scarborough, collapsed in the pits after 70 laps and died from heat prostration.

Vukovich took an early lead and held it for almost the entire race. He watched as 25 cars dropped out, many from heat-related problems. By the midway point, he had already lapped the 2-3-4 cars, driven by Art Cross, Sam Hanks, and McGrath. It had been nearly a quarter-century since a driver had won so handily. When Vukovich glided down Victory Lane, he did not look like the winner in a grueling battle for survival. The "Mad Russian" seemed like he had just come from a sunny day at the beach.

Winner: Troy Ruttman
Car: Kuzma
Speed: 128.9 mph
  2. Jim Rathmann
  3. Sam Hanks
  4. Duane Carter
  5. Art Cross

Winner: Bill Vukovich
Car: Fuel Injection Special
Speed: 128.7 mph
  2. Art Cross
  3. Sam Hanks
  4. Fred Agabashian
  5. Jack McGrath

1953

The highly anticipated duel between Troy Ruttman and Bill Vukovich never came to pass in 1953. While Vukovich sloshed through the rain to win the pole position in qualifying, Ruttman could only watch longingly from pit row. He was unable to defend his title because of an injured arm. Fred Agabashian and Jack McGrath were figured to give Vukovich the most trouble.

On race day, the temperature soared above 90 degrees, and would reach 130 on the track thermometer. It was a day for sturdy cars and young men with lots of sta-

1954

Bill Vukovich came to Indy in the spring of 1954 as auto racing's uncrowned king. He was the nation's hottest young driver, and needed only another Indy win to make it "official." The other drivers seemed resigned to play follow the leader until Vukovich finished a disappointing 19th in the time trials. This surprising development thrust pole-winner Jack McGrath (the first to crack the 140 mph mark) into the favorite's role, along with Jimmy Bryan, Jimmy Daywalt, and Troy Ruttman, who was healthy and hungry again.

GREAT DRIVER: BILL VUKOVICH

Normally, race car drivers have to work their way up a long ladder—with success at each rung—before getting to compete in the Indy 500. Bill Vukovich was a 30-something driver who had not progressed beyond the midget car circuit. He was hired as a substitute for the 1950 and 1951 races, and drove surprisingly well each time. In 1952, Vukovich was hired to drive Howard Keck's Kurtis roadster, and he came within eight laps of winning the race before his steering failed and he hit the wall in turn 3. Nonetheless, for a California dirt-track racer, $7,500 was a darn good payday.

Bill Vukovich smiles after winning the 1953 race. Few drivers have ever dominated the field as he did that year.

Vukovich drove for Keck again at Indy in 1953, on a miserably hot day. He was one of only five drivers who went start-to-finish without relief. He also led the race for all but five laps. When the checkered flag came down, the "Mad Russian" was the toast of the town. In 1954, he repeated as Indy 500 champ, again winning with ease.

Vukovich was not looking for a long career in Indy car racing. In fact, he spent most of his winnings on a couple of gas stations, at which he worked regular hours during the year. His plan was to live simply, and return to the Brickyard each year, where he could collect a big purse with a good finish. Sure enough, in 1955, he was out ahead of the pack at Indy again after 55 laps.

Suddenly, Rodger Ward broke an axle, causing Johnny Boyd to swerve in front of Vukovich. With little time to maneuver, Vukovich had no choice but to run over Boyd's tire and hope for the best. Vukovich's car was launched into the air, and it cartwheeled off the track, landing upside down, bursting into flames, and crushing his skull.

So ended the most dominant stretch ever enjoyed by an Indy driver. Between 1952 and 1955, Vukovich led nearly 500 laps, and was in position to win all four races. Bad luck robbed him of his first chance at Indy glory, then took his life three years later.

As expected, McGrath and Bryan opened up an early lead. They were joined briefly by Ruttman, who had to make a stop after shredding a tire. The crowd watched and waited for Vukovich to make his move, and were surprised by his cautious driving. The defending champ had decided to let the leaders duke it out—for now, at least.

Around the halfway mark, Vukovich sensed that McGrath was beginning to struggle. He worked his way through the pack and passed McGrath. Bryan was the next driver in Vukovich's crosshairs. The two cars dueled for the lead over several laps, until Bryan's car began to fall apart from the stress. First the shock absorbers buckled, then the brakes wore out. An oil leak caused searing hot oil to burn his left leg. Finally, Bryan's car started shaking violently. The former Air Force cadet toughed it out (his body was bruised from head to toe by the end of the day) and somehow managed to hold on to second place. Vukovich took the checkered flag with worn tires and a tired smile. Luck seemed to be squarely on his side.

Winner: Bill Vukovich
Car: Fuel Injection Special
Speed: 130.8 mph
    2. Jimmy Bryan
    3. Jack McGrath
    4. Troy Ruttman
    5. Mike Nazaruk

1955

Death hung in the air before, during, and after the 1955 Indy 500. The beloved Wilbur Shaw, who ushered in the modern era at the Brickyard, had perished in a plane crash the previous October. Owner Tony Hulman added Shaw's job to his already long list of responsibilities, including that of official "starter" on race day. Although Jerry Hoyt and Tony Bettenhausen had made tremendous qualifying runs under windy conditions, the hands-down favorite to win for a third straight year was Bill Vukovich.

Starting from the fifth position, Vukovich sped past Jack McGrath on the fourth lap and took the lead. The veteran shadowed the young champion for the next 100 miles, but Vukovich managed to hold on to first place. On Lap 56, however, trouble developed. A half-dozen cars tangled on the back stretch, including Johnny Boyd's futuristic Sumar. Boyd veered into Vukovich, who lost control and—to the horror of everyone in the stands—bounced end-over-end right off the track. By the time medics reached Vukovich, he was dead.

Everyone was numb from the shock, but once the debris was cleaned from the pavement, there was still a race to be run. Jimmy Bryan, the reigning USAC champ, led until lap 90, when a broken fuel pump ended his day. That left Art Cross, Don Freeland, and Bob Sweikert to tussle for the lead. Cross appeared to be the front runner until his engine blew with 75 miles to go. Freeland was next to seize the advantage, but transmission problems sidelined him 10 laps later. By process of elimination, Sweikert was the new leader. He had two laps on Bettenhausen, and maintained that advantage until the checkered flag dropped. It was a sweet victory for Sweikert, but a sad time for racing. The loss of Vukovich dampened enthusiasm for the sport for many months.

THE GOLDEN YEARS • 43

> **Winner: Bob Sweikert**
> Car: John Zink Special
> Speed: 128.2 mph
> > 2. Tony Bettenhausen
> > 3. Jim Davies
> > 4. Johnny Thomson
> > 5. Walt Faulkner

1956

There were all sorts of changes at Indy for the 1956 race. A new layer of asphalt had been added to the track, and this pushed qualifying speeds well into the 140s. A racing museum was added to the complex, and it proved an enormous hit with fans. Also, the familiar AAA logos were gone, replaced by USAC signage. The American Automobile Association had sanctioned the Indy 500 since its first running, but had pulled out of racing after 1955. AAA had long been criticized for the message it was sending to everyday drivers by supporting dangerous, high-speed races. The death of Bill Vukovich and a crash at the French Grand Prix that killed 83 spectators was enough to force the AAA to make a choice. Tony Hulman quickly arranged for the United States Auto Club to sanction the Indy 500.

Pat Flaherty claimed the pole position, then had to wait anxiously with the other 32 qualifiers as torrential rains rolled into Indianapolis and submerged the track 72 hours before race day. The cleanup crews did a commendable job, but conditions were still a little worrisome when the race went off as scheduled on Sunday. Flaherty, driving a beautifully designed car built by A.J. Watson, streaked around the turns, while others cautiously felt their way. He was challenged

briefly by Paul Russo, who was driving a powerful Novi Vespa (the lone car that day not powered by an Offy engine). Russo screamed past Flaherty at 180 mph, but blew a tire 10 laps later, skidded on the damp pavement, and crashed into the wall.

Several more crashes were attributed to the slick track, including ones involving Tony Bettenhausen, Jimmy Daywalt, and Troy Ruttman. Meanwhile, Flaherty held off challenges from Dick Rathmann, Pat O'Connor, and Sam Hanks for what seemed to be an easy win. Only after he crossed the finish line did he realize how narrow his margin really was—as he entered Victory Lane, his engine gave out.

> **Winner: Pat Flaherty**
> Car: John Zink Special
> Speed: 128.5 mph
> > 2. Sam Hanks
> > 3. Don Freeland
> > 4. Johnnie Parsons
> > 5. Dick Rathmann

1957

Fans arriving at the brickyard for the 1957 race were greeted by a modern marvel. The track's famous pagoda-style timing tower was gone, replaced by a steel-and-glass control tower that was surrounded by a brand new section of grandstand. Down on the track, teams luxuriated in a widened and improved pit area. Pat O'Connor nipped rookie Eddie Sachs in qualifying, but the consensus was that this could be anyone's race.

The starting field dropped from 33 to 31 before the green flag came down. During the "parade lap," a nervous rookie named

Indy's famous "Pagoda" timing tower, which graced the track until 1957.

Elmer George smashed into the back of Eddie Russo's car and both were knocked out of the race. When the real driving started, Troy Ruttman, Paul Russo, and O'Connor grabbed the lead. Ruttman's car overheated and he dropped out, then lengthy pit stops slowed the other two. Sam Hanks grabbed first place on the 37th lap, and held it until lap 111 when Jim Rathmann (Dick Rathmann's brother) came out of nowhere to pass him while he was in the pits.

Rathmann's own pit crew had been working miracles all day, helping him go from 32nd place to first. Combined with his hard-charging style, it looked as if he were destined for victory. The 42-year-old Hanks had bided his time and waited for the perfect opportunity to pass Rathmann. He squeezed by him with 34 laps to go and barely held him off the rest of the way to

win by 22 seconds. As Hanks clutched the Borg-Warner trophy in Victory Lane, the veteran tearfully announced his retirement.

Winner: Sam Hanks
Car: Belond Exhaust Special
Speed: 135.6 mph
   2. Jim Rathmann
   3. Jimmy Bryan
   4. Paul Russo
   5. Andy Linden

1958

The victory by Sam Hanks in 1957 touched off a mini-revolution at Indy. For years, auto racing designers had been moving their engines to the left side of the car in order to fight the effects of centrifugal force when taking turns at high speed. Hanks's car, built by George Salih, had its engine tilted over to the left on a 72 degree angle. This put even more weight on that side, and also lowered the profile of the car to 21 inches, which cut down on wind resistance. These ideas were echoed in most of the 1958 entries. Adding to the new look of the race were eight first-time qualifiers, including Jerry Unser and A.J. Foyt. Dick Rathmann claimed the pole, with Ed Elisian, Jimmy Reece, Bob Veith, Pat O'Connor, Johnnie Parsons, and Jimmy Bryan behind him.

The race was not even a lap old when Rathmann and Elisian decided to play chicken heading into turn 3. They collided, triggering a 15-car crash that put eight cars out of the race. Unser dislocated his shoulder when his car rolled over the wall; O'Connor was crushed to death when his Sumar Special flipped on top of him. When the caution flag was lifted, Tony Bettenhausen, George Amick, Sachs, Bryan and Foyt were in the lead pack. This developed into a two-way battle between Amick and Sachs, two of the youngest drivers at Indy, until Sachs dropped out with engine problems. Bryan, driving a Belond AP Special designed by Salih, crept up on Amick and started applying pressure on the rookie. Amick did his best to hold off Bryan, but experience won out over exuberance and Bryan beat him by less than 30 seconds.

Winner: Jimmy Bryan,
Car: Belond AP Special
Speed: 133.8 mph
　　2. George Amick
　　3. Johnny Boyd
　　4. Tony Bettenhausen
　　5. Jim Rathmann

Jimmy Bryan, the 1958 winner. The rollbar behind his helmet became mandatory on all cars in 1959, after Pat O'Connor was killed.

1959

A lot of the safety devices and equipment we see today in Indy cars probably seem like "no-brainers." Unfortunately, most of these design changes were not adopted until many people were badly hurt or killed. Fire-resistant suits, for instance, did not become mandatory until after the 1959 race—too late for Jerry Unser, who suffered fatal burns during a pre-race practice run. His younger brothers, Bobby and Al, were left to carry on the family name. The death of Pat O'Connor a year earlier convinced Indy officials to make rollbars mandatory on all cars—just in time for Tony Bettenhausen, who walked away from a nasty crash during qualifying.

When the green flag dropped, all eyes were on the 20th-place car, designed by visionary George Salih and driven by defending champion, Jimmy Bryan. Incredibly, his camshaft snapped after just one lap and he was out of the race. Attention then turned to the lead pack, which included Johnny Thomson, Eddie Sachs, the Rathmann brothers, Bobby Grim, and Rodger Ward. A World War II fighter pilot, Ward was not very serious about his profession when he first came to Indy in the early 1950s. In fact, some blamed his sloppy driving for the accident that killed Bill Vukovich. Ward had since changed his ways and was now a respected veteran.

The field thinned out after a crack-up on lap 45, and Pat Flaherty joined the leaders. By the midway point, the race was still very much up for grabs. Flaherty, the 1956 winner, seemed to have the inside track. But with 37 laps to go he spun out into the pit area. Ward, who had been at or near the front for most of the race, darted into the pits for his final stop while they were still cleaning up Flaherty's mess. Ward pulled back on to the track after a lightning-fast pit, and waited for the two cars still in front of him (driven by Thomson and Jim Rathmann) to make their final pit stops. Neither crew matched Ward's, and the two leaders were suddenly followers, as Ward whooshed by them. He won by 23 seconds. After the race, mechanic A.J. Watson inspected the engine and discovered a broken piston plug. Had Ward needed to circle the track one more time, he probably would not have made it.

> **Winner: Rodger Ward**
> Car: Leader Card 500 Roadster
> Speed: 135.9 mph
>   2. Jim Rathmann
>   3. Johnny Thomson
>   4. Tony Bettenhausen
>   5. Paul Goldsmith

1959 champion Rodger Ward (left) welcomes rookie Jack Brabham to Indy in 1961.

1960

Death visited the Brickyard again in 1960, but this time the accident occurred in the stands. Just before the race, a temporary grandstand collapsed, killing two spectators and injuring scores of people. By comparison, the race itself seemed like a leisurely Sunday drive. Favorites Rodger Ward, Jim Rathmann, Eddie Sachs, and Troy Ruttman all figured in the early action, swapping the lead and trying to out-pit one another. This group, with Johnny Thomson trailing, established itself by mid-race.

Slowly but surely, Ward and Rathmann pulled away. They dueled for the final 100 miles, and in the last 31 laps, they traded the lead eight times. Thomson, still within striking range, dropped back with 10 laps left due to engine trouble. The smart money was on Ward to repeat his 1959 victory, but a badly worn tire hampered him down the stretch. With three laps remaining, Rathmann pulled ahead for good. It was Indy car racing at its very best.

> **Winner: Jim Rathmann**
> Car: Ken-Paul Special
> Speed: 138.8 mph
>   2. Rodger Ward
>   3. Paul Goldsmith
>   4. Don Branson
>   5. Johnny Thomson

1961

The Indianapolis 500 marked its 50th birthday in 1961. To celebrate, Tony Hulman erected a double-decker grandstand and raised the prize money total to $400,000. The festive mood was dampened, however, when Tony Bettenhausen—a racing fixture for more than a decade—was killed during a practice run. Despite this loss, the starting grid was a good one. Eddie Sachs won the pole, Rodger Ward and Troy Ruttman were looking for their second Indy wins, and Australian Grand Prix star Jack Brabham was in the field for the first time. Another rookie from the Grand Prix circuit was Parnelli Jones. And rising stars Sachs, A.J. Foyt, and Jim Hurtubise now had enough experience to win.

Hurtubise seized the early advantage, but Jones took it from him while he was in the pits. Brabham, at the wheel of his light, slick-handling Cooper-Climax, stayed within striking range. As the race approached the midway point, Jones faded, while Foyt slipped past Hurtubise and Brabham into first place. Ruttmann made a spirited charge, but destroyed his clutch in the process.

Foyt maintained his advantage, and next had to hold off Ward and Sachs. For the rest of the race, all eyes were trained on this trio. Foyt dabbled with disaster during what should have been his final pit stop. When a problem developed during refueling, he decided to pull back on the track and deal with it later. On lap 184, his tank nearly empty, Foyt steered back into the pits for a final splash. This gave Sachs the chance he needed, and he assumed control of first place, with Ward still running third. Sachs was looking golden until he felt his right rear tire starting to disintegrate. For a few laps he thought he might make it to the finish line, but with less than 10 miles to go

Eddie Sachs's roadster challenges Jack Brabham's rear-engine Copper-Climax in action from the 1961 race.

GREAT DRIVER: A.J. FOYT

"The Brickyard" comes by its name honestly. Superstar A.J. Foyt poses on an exposed section of the original track in 1961.

The most successful American racer, both on and off the track, would have to be A.J. Foyt. Besides his four Indy 500 victories (1961, 1964, 1967, and 1977), the Houston-born Foyt retired with 67 Indy car victories and six national driving championships. Foyt won seven NASCAR events, 41 USAC stock-car races, and captured 21 midget titles during the 1950s. In 1968, he became one of only three men ever to win major events on oval tracks, dirt tracks, and road courses. He is also the only driver to win the Indy 500, Daytona 500, and 24 Hours of Le Mans.

The career choices a driver makes can change the course of racing history, and Foyt is perhaps the best example of that. In 1959, just as he was about to burst upon the American racing scene, he received a lucrative offer to become a Formula One driver in Europe. Foyt turned it down, and a year later he was driving down Victory Lane at the Brickyard.

there was almost no rubber left on the tread. Sachs pitted for a tire change, and Foyt streaked past him before he could get back out. Foyt took the checkered flag by a mere nine seconds in a thrilling finish.

> **Winner: A. J. Foyt**
> **Car: Bowes Seal Fast Special**
> **Speed: 139.1 mph**
>   2. Eddie Sachs
>   3. Rodger Ward
>   4. Shorty Templeman
>   5. Al Keller

1962

The Brickyard got faster in 1962, thanks to fewer bricks. The long strip in front of the grandstand was paved over, leaving only a thin band of the track's original surface at the start-finish line. Parnelli Jones eclipsed the 150 mph barrier in qualifying, and everyone agreed that this year's winner would probably end up averaging more than 140 mph. Next to Jones in the front row was Rodger Ward. Ward's teammate, Len Sutton, also ran fast in qualifying, and was considered a dark horse to win the race. A.J. Foyt, the defending champ, qualified fifth and had his sights set on back-to-back victories. Starting eighth was rookie Dan Gurney. He was piloting a light, ground-hugging

machine designed by automotive innovator Mickey Thompson. It was only the second qualifying car of the 1960s that was not powered by the dominant Offy engine.

Jones exploded off the line when the green flag dropped, and Foyt tried gallantly to keep pace. During a pit stop on lap 70, Foyt's engine shut down and his crew had to push-start his car to get him back on the track. He eventually had to drop out. Gurney bowed out after 91 laps when his rear end began to come apart.

Jones was looking unbeatable, but he had one problem—his brakes were shot. Whenever he pitted, his crew had to set up a wall of tires to stop him. After a couple of stops, the extra time this cost him opened the door for Ward, who grabbed the lead and held it for the final 200 miles. As the fans predicted, Ward's speed averaged over 140 mph. With a new era of car and engine design on the horizon, it would not be long before Indy drivers reached the 150 mph plateau.

> **Winner: Rodger Ward**
> **Car: Leader Card 500**
> **Speed: 140.3 mph**
>   2. Len Sutton
>   3. Eddie Sachs
>   4. Don Davis
>   5. Bobby Marshman

CHAPTER 4

THE MODERN ERA

1963

A move was afoot to rethink the Indy car. Racing engineers on both sides of the Atlantic were coming to the conclusion that moving the engine behind the driver, lowering the chassis profile, and widening the wheels produced a lighter, faster, more responsive car. The old tube-shaped racer was already "flattening out" each year; soon Indy cars would look more like doorstops than cigars.

Jim Clark, America's premier Formula One driver, showed up with a rear-engine Ford-powered Lotus that looked like a toy next to the competition. Other drivers claimed the car was unsafe, and that Clark was too inexperienced to survive 200 laps. Parnelli Jones, who had the fastest car in qualifying, nonetheless seemed intrigued with the Lotus. Always on the cutting edge, Jones recognized before his fellow Indy drivers that he was getting a peek at the future.

Jim Hurtubise, driving a Novi-powered Kurtis sponsored by the Tropicana Hotel, set the tone early with a charge to the front of the pack. Jones wasted no time in regaining the lead. He held it through 40 laps, with Clark and Dan Gurney (also in a Lotus) right on his tail. When Jones made a pit stop, this pair assumed command and Clark held the lead until he pitted at the midway point.

Jones, now back in front, held off a challenge by A.J. Foyt. With 20 laps to go, however, his car began coughing out smoke. Jones determined it was just a small oil leak—nothing that would prevent him from finishing. He continued circling the track at high speed, only to see Eddie Sachs coming up fast. On the 182nd lap, with Sachs bearing down on him, Jones began to leak oil onto the track. Sachs hit a slick patch and careened into the wall. Race officials debated whether to "black flag" Jones (pull him off the track) but decided he did not present a hazard to the other drivers. It was a controversial call, for by the time caution was lifted, no one could catch him. Had Jones been removed, Clark (the second-place finisher) would have won. When Sachs confronted Jones at the traditional Monday drivers' luncheon and claimed he did not deserve to win the race, Jones punched him in the nose.

> **Winner: Parnelli Jones**
> Car: Agajanian Willard Batt
> Speed: 143.1
> 2. Jim Clark
> 3. A. J. Foyt
> 4. Rodger Ward
> 5. Don Branson

1964

Were rear-engine cars truly the future of Indy? Jim Clark's grand performance in 1963 seemed to suggest so. The debate raged all winter and right into spring—until trend-setting owner A.J. Watson showed up at Indy in 1964 with a pair of rear-engine beauties. To most, this signalled a changing of the guard. Any remaining skeptics were left to explain why, on race day, the entire front row was made up of rear-engine machines. Clark and Bobby Marshman (both in Lotuses) and Rodger Ward (in one of Watson's cars) were the top three qualifiers. A.J. Foyt and Parnelli Jones, still driving with front-mounted engines, were also among the favorites.

The race began as expected, with Clark getting off the mark quickly and carving out a small lead. On lap 2, however, chaos erupted when rookie Dave MacDonald's car skidded into the wall with a full tank and exploded. Eddie Sachs, also loaded with high-powered fuel, hit MacDonald and created a second fireball. Both drivers were completely consumed by the flames, and for the first time ever, the race was halted completely so the wreckage and bodies could be dragged away.

When the race resumed, Clark and Marshman battled for first. But 50 laps later

both men were out with mechanical woes. Jones was leading at this point, but his time in front did not last long, either. After a pit stop, his fuel tank caught fire and he had to run for his life. Foyt, Ward, and Dan Gurney now charged ahead, with Foyt pulling in front and building a healthy advantage. Gurney dropped out with a bad tire, and Ward had to take on extra fuel, which slowed him down and prevented him from closing on Foyt. The 1961 winner took his second checkered flag a full lap ahead of Ward.

> **Winner: A. J. Foyt**
> Car: Sheraton-Thompson
> Speed: 147.3 mph
> 2. Rodger Ward
> 3. Lloyd Ruby
> 4. Johnny White
> 5. Johnny Boyd

1965

The smoke had barely cleared from the horrible 1964 crash when USAC officials announced sweeping changes in gas and gas-tank safety. No longer would highly combustible fuel mixes be allowed, and tanks would have to be virtually puncture-proof. Qualification for the 1965 race, during which several drivers topped 160 mph, passed without incident. The 33-car field featured 27 rear-engine models and 11 rookies, including Mario Andretti, Gordon Johncock, and Al Unser, whose brother Bobby had been running at Indy since 1963. A.J. Foyt was the race favorite, along with Jim Clark, who was hoping for some good luck for a change. Dan Gurney and Parnelli Jones, always dangerous, were positioned in the second row.

Foyt and Clark pulled away from the pack almost immediately, and for the next 66 laps they traded the lead like a couple of kids swapping baseball cards. Foyt gained an advantage when Clark hit the pits, but Clark ended up with the edge after Foyt's crew made him endure an excruciating 44-second stop of his own. Foyt got back into the race before Andretti, Jones, Johncock, and Al Unser could catch him, but was forced to stop when his gear box broke.

Although Jones made a spirited charge, Clark was just too far ahead. He won by two laps, and became the first overseas driver to take home the Borg-Warner trophy since World War I. Clark's average speed was an awe-inspiring 150 mph. It had not been that long since 150 was considered an outstanding qualifying speed!

Winner: Jim Clark
Car: Lotus-Ford
Speed: 150.7 mph
   2. Parnelli Jones
   3. Mario Andretti
   4. Al Miller
   5. Gordon Johncock

1966

Thanks to the 1965 victory by Grand Prix star Jim Clark, the Brickyard welcomed two of the top Formula One drivers, Scotland's Jackie Stewart and England's Graham Hill. They were the wild cards in a field that included top qualifiers Mario Andretti, George Snider, Parnelli Jones, and Lloyd Ruby.

For the second time in three years, the race was halted almost as soon as it started. A huge pileup (this time there were no serious injuries) took one-third of the drivers out of the race, including A.J. Foyt, Dan Gurney, and NASCAR star Cale Yarborough. When the remaining drivers got the green light, a second accident caused more delays!

Finally, the race got off and Andretti roared into the lead. The super-aggressive pole-sitter threatened to run away with things until a blown valve sent smoke belching from his engine and knocked him out of the race. Clark took the lead briefly before giving way to Ruby, who maintained his advantage despite a terrifying spinout. By mid-race, Stewart and Al Unser had joined the fun.

Ruby faded when his engine began leaking oil, and Stewart took control. Unser mounted a brief challenge, which ended when he hit the wall on the 161st lap. With dreams of transatlantic glory dancing in his head, Stewart prepared himself for a fantastic finish. With 25 laps to go, he had a big lead on Hill, Clark, Jim McElreath, and Gordon Johncock. With 10 laps remaining, Stewart was still well out in front. Then without warning, his oil pressure bottomed out and his engine simply failed. Hill cruised to an easy win—the second in a row for a foreign driver.

Winner: Graham Hill
Car: American Red Ball Special
Speed: 144.3 mph
   2. Jim Clark
   3. Jim McElreath
   4. Gordon Johncock
   5. Mel Kenyon

1967

Two nights before the 1967 Indy 500, A.J. Foyt had a dream. In it, he had to do some quick thinking on the final lap to take the checkered flag. Foyt knew that to make this dream come true, he would have to beat the top three qualifiers—Mario Andretti, Dan Gurney, and Gordon Johncock. The brash, confident Texan would also have to contend with some other formidable foes, including the smooth-talking trio of Jackie Stewart, Graham Hill, and Jim Clark.

Parnelli Jones, starting in the second row, floored it when the green flag dropped and sped right past a startled Andretti. A bad clutch sent the pole-sitter into the pits, but he lucked out when a steady downpour began to soak the track. Fifteen minutes later, officials decided to postpone the race.

A day later, when the race was restarted, Andretti's luck ran out for good when he lost a tire on lap 58 and was done for the day. He was not the first of the favorites to fall. Clark and Hill had both called it quits earlier when they suffered burned pistons. Later in the race, Gurney suffered the same fate.

In the meantime, Foyt patiently shadowed Jones, waiting for him to falter. After 130 laps, Jones made his second pit stop and Foyt shot by him. Jones returned the favor when Foyt had to refuel. With less than four laps to go, Foyt's patience paid off when Jones felt his transmission slip. He veered into the pits, leaving Foyt all alone to win the race. On the final lap, Chuck Hulse, Carl Williams, and Bobby Grim got tangled up in front of Foyt. He slowed down, spotted a path through the wreckage, and took the checkered flag for his third Indy 500 victory. It was literally a dream come true!

Winner: A. J. Foyt
Car: Sheraton-Thompson
Speed: 151.2 mph
2. Al Unser
3. Joe Leonard
4. Denis Hulme
5. Jim McElreath

1968

Andy Granatelli had been entering cars at Indy since the late 1940s, but not until the 1960s was he recognized as a racing visionary. The Chicago-based owner followed a simple rule: if everyone else was doing it one way, there had to be a better way. Sometimes this approach worked, and sometimes it blew up in his face. In 1968, Granatelli planned to hit the Brickyard with a trio of sleek Lotuses powered by futuristic turbine engines, driven by three great stars: Parnelli Jones, Graham Hill, and Jackie Stewart. Granatelli aimed to shake things up, but instead he was the one receiving a jolt when Stewart pulled out because of a broken wrist. Then Jones quit when USAC issued new restrictions that he felt would keep his car out of Victory Lane. Desperate for drivers, Granatelli tabbed "Pelican Joe" Leonard, who promptly went out and won the pole position with the eye-popping speed of 171 mph. Sitting next to him in the front row was Hill, who also qualified at 171 mph. Art Pollard, Granatelli's other replacement, started 11th.

Leonard grabbed the early lead, only to relinquish this advantage to Bobby Unser on the ninth lap. This pair raced 1-2 for more than an hour, until Lloyd Ruby passed them both during a dual pit stop. When they returned to the race, they were joined by Hill and Dan Gurney. Things were setting up nicely for Granatelli. He had two cars in contention, while several top drivers—including Mario Andretti, A.J. Foyt, Al Unser, and Gordon Johncock—were already out of the race.

On lap 110, Hill hit the wall, leaving only two Granatelli drivers in the race. But Leonard was looking good, as both Ruby and Bobby Unser were experiencing mechanical problems. Unser's crew got him back to full speed quickly, and he and Leonard renewed their earlier head-to-head battle. With ten laps remaining, Leonard, clinging to a slim lead, felt his engine suddenly stall due to a broken fuel shaft. Minutes earlier, the same thing had happened to Pollard's car. A pleasantly surprised Unser crossed the finish line as a stunned Granatelli stood helplessly in the pits.

> **Winner: Bobby Unser**
> Car: Rislone
> Speed: 152.9 mph
>   2. Dan Gurney
>   3. Mel Kenyon
>   4. Denis Hulme
>   5. Lloyd Ruby

1969

Andy Granatelli's dream was to be known as "Mr. 500." He had plowed the profits from his successful STP engine treatment into racing, investing in cutting-edge technology and great drivers. In 1969, Granatelli hired the fearless Mario Andretti to drive his new wedge-shaped Lotus. Imagine his dismay when Andretti destroyed the car in practice! Undaunted, An-

dretti climbed into the same Ford-powered Hawk with which he had won the pole position in 1967 and proceeded to qualify second, right behind A.J. Foyt. Bobby Unser shared the front row with these two; Gordon Johncock, Roger McCluskey, and Mark Donohue were positioned right behind them. Donohue made for good copy. A former polio victim and formally trained engineer, he was a superb road racer making his first start at Indy at the age of 32.

Andretti and Foyt sprinted to a solid lead in the first few laps, while Unser found his car hard to handle and dropped off the pace. A quarter of the way through the race, the leaders pitted and Foyt's crew helped him gain 15 seconds on Andretti. Foyt looked to extend his lead, but his engine overheated, leaving Andretti in full command. Dan Gurney mounted a spirited challenge, but never really got close. Andretti sped across the finish line and rolled down Victory Lane—where a jubilant Granatelli planted a big kiss on his cheek.

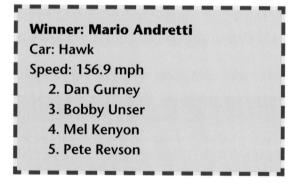

> **Winner: Mario Andretti**
> Car: Hawk
> Speed: 156.9 mph
>   2. Dan Gurney
>   3. Bobby Unser
>   4. Mel Kenyon
>   5. Pete Revson

1970

Track historians often argue about the "best-ever" starting field for the Indy 500. Many pick the 1970 race, which featured all-time greats Mario Andretti, Jack Brabham, Mark Donohue, A.J. Foyt, Dan Gurney, Gordon

GREAT DRIVER: MARIO ANDRETTI

In a sport where rags-to-riches stories are not uncommon, Mario Andretti's stands above the rest. He and twin brother, Aldo, were born in Italy during World War II. The Andretti family survived the war, but had to flee their home—now part of Croatia—after Communist rule was established in 1945. They spent the next seven years living in squalor at a displaced persons camp in Tuscany.

Mario and Aldo spent their days building go-carts out of scrap wood, and racing them down the steep hills where they lived. They also followed the exploits of Italy's famous Grand Prix champion, Alberto Ascari. By the time the family emigrated to the United States in 1955, both brothers were bitten by the racing bug.

A few years later the brothers—unbeknownst to their parents—bought an 11-year-old Hudson and began racing secretly on the dirt tracks near their new home in Nazareth, Pennsylvania. They took turns, with one driving and the other serving as pit crew. A terrible crash ended Aldo's career, but Mario kept racing. He won races in midgets, sprint cars, champ cars, sports cars, and stock cars—on every surface imaginable. Mario Andretti was what they call a "natural."

Andretti was offered his first ride at Indy in 1964, but turned it down; he had a bad feeling about the car. The driver who took that ride, Eddie Sachs, was killed in a crash. A year later he felt he was ready, and finished third to win Indy Rookie of the Year. Only five years later, in 1969, Andretti won the Indy 500.

Andretti continued driving different cars in different races, and continued winning. He was named USAC Driver of the Year in 1967, 1978, and 1984—the only person ever to win the award in three different decades. Andretti became the oldest pole winner (52) at Indy in 1992, and in 1993 he became the oldest driver to win an Indy car race when he took the checkered flag at the Phoenix International Raceway.

During his long career, Andretti also won the Daytona 500, the Pike's Peak Hill Climb, and Grand Prix races in eight foreign countries. He was also the Formula One champion in 1978. Although Andretti never won the Indy 500 again, he was almost always among the leaders, and figured into many thrilling finishes at the Brickyard.

Johncock, Johnny Rutherford, Al and Bobby Unser, as well as NASCAR greats Donnie Allison and LeeRoy Yarbrough. The fans certainly seemed to agree. They piled into the Brickyard in record numbers. Al Unser, Rutherford, and Foyt started in the front row, with Unser driving a beautiful Ford-powered Johnny Lightning Colt for Parnelli Jones, who was now an owner. With prize money, for the first time, totaling more than $1 million, the anticipation was at a fever pitch when the familiar call of "Gentlemen, start your engines" boomed from the public address system.

Rutherford snuck past Unser after the green flag dropped, but the pole-sitter re-

The front row for the 1970 Indy 500 is a Who's Who of American auto racing: (left to right) A.J. Foyt, Johnny Rutherford, and Al Unser.

gained the lead and held it for more than 100 miles before his first pit stop. Foyt briefly held the top spot until he, too, pitted. This opened the door for Lloyd Ruby, a fan favorite who had skillfully snaked his way from 25th to first. When his car started leaking oil, however, he was flagged to the pits and later had to leave the race when his car caught fire. Donohue also was in the lead for a while, but eventually Unser returned to the front of the pack. After fending off a second challenge from Donohue, Unser opened up a hefty lead in the second half of the race. He made his final pit stop, then eased up on the gas and cruised to a comfortable victory. He and Bobby were the first brothers to notch Indy wins.

Winner: Al Unser
Car: Johnny Lightning Colt
Speed: 155.7 mph
2. Mark Donohue
3. Dan Gurney
4. Donnie Allison
5. Jim McElreath

1971

The high interest in the Indianapolis 500 before, during, and after the 1970 race convinced television executives that it was more than just a midwestern phenomenon. For the 1971 Indy 500, ABC bought the broadcast rights and sent its top camera crews and announcers to the Brickyard to televise the race on tape delay. Pete Revson, heir to the Revlon cosmetics empire, won the pole with a qualifying speed of 178.7 mph. His car was one of three wedge-shaped turbocharged M16 McLarens to qualify in the top four—the other two were driven by Mark Donohue and Denny Hulme. These cars would be watched closely, for they incorporated many features from European Formula One racers. Defending champ Al Unser, in his Johnny Lightning started fifth.

After the parade lap, Donohue raced to an early lead, but hardly anyone noticed. The pace car, driven by a local auto dealer, crashed into the photographer's stand, injuring 29 people. Donohue held the top spot for most of the first 66 laps, until a broken transmission ended his day. Bobby Unser, driving a wedge-shaped Eagle for Dan Gurney, pulled into first place, with his brother Al right behind him. It was the first time brothers had ever run 1-2 at the Brickyard. At the midway point, the two were still jockeying for position, with Lloyd Ruby lurking right behind them. On lap 113, Al took the lead from his brother for good.

The race continued without incident for 45 minutes, until Mike Mosley's car lost a tire on turn 4, flipped over and caught fire. Gary Bettenhausen stopped and helped to pull Mosley from the flaming wreckage, saving his life. He then hopped back in his car and finished the race (10th). In the confusion, Bobby Unser slammed into the wall trying to avoid Mosley, and was out of the race. That left Revson and Foyt to catch his little brother, but Al pulled away once the caution flag was lifted and won the race for the second consecutive year. To casual fans, it looked like the classic Indy car was here to

stay. But to racing insiders, the fine performances of the Formula One-style vehicles suggested a major change was on the horizon.

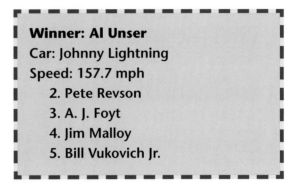

Winner: Al Unser
Car: Johnny Lightning
Speed: 157.7 mph
　2. Pete Revson
　3. A. J. Foyt
　4. Jim Malloy
　5. Bill Vukovich Jr.

1972

The look of Indy cars changed dramatically from 1971 to 1972, as each team did indeed embrace design changes inspired by Formula One. Every single qualifier had front and rear air foils, which "pushed" the car down as air flowed over them. This increased the bite of the tires, which improved speed and handling. Fans who came to the Brickyard to watch qualifying were dumbstruck by the speeds that flashed up on the board. Prior to 1972, no qualifier had ever gone faster than 178 mph. Suddenly, everyone was qualifying in the 180s and 190s. The pole sitter, Bobby Unser, turned in a speed of 195.9 mph! He shared the front row with Pete Revson and Mark Donohue.

Racing and qualifying can be two very different things. This became clear in the first half-hour, when both Unser and Revson broke down. Gary Bettenhausen, Jerry Grant, and Donohue eventually established themselves as the trio to beat, holding off all challengers until lap 25. That is, when Bettenhausen developed engine problems and faded from contention. Grant led Donohue, however he needed a tire change. He darted

GREAT DRIVER: MARK DONOHUE

Mark Donohue poses with the car he drove to victory in 1972.

No driver ever combined intelligence and versatility as well as Mark Donohue, the winner of the 1972 Indy 500. He graduated from Brown University in 1959 with a degree in mechanical engineering, and entered races on the weekends for fun. Soon he was winning events all over the country, and by 1966 he decided to change careers and become a professional racer.

Starting as a test-driver for Roger Penske, Donohue quickly became one of his top competitors. His engineering background, competitive spirit, and amazing ability to stay calm during races enabled him to win in any car he drove. Prior to his first Indy 500 start in 1969, Donohue piloted sports cars, sedans, and stock cars to victory. Later in his career he mastered the Porsche 917-10, one of the most dangerous and powerful cars ever conceived.

Donohue finished seventh in his first run at the Brickyard to win Rookie of the Year honors. His quiet demeanor earned him the nickname "Captain Nice," while his science background made the other drivers a little jealous. Donohue finished second in 1970, and would have won in 1971 had his gearbox held out. In 1972, he and Penske entered a car that was slightly underpowered but built to go the distance. In a masterful driving job, Donohue took the checkered flag and set a new speed record at 163 mph.

Donohue retired to build Formula One cars for Pete Revson, but when Revson was killed he came out of retirement in 1974 to compete. A year later, during a pre-race warmup for the Austrian Grand Prix, Donohue blew a front tire and crashed hard. He appeared okay, except for a bad headache. On his way to have it checked out at the hospital, Donohue lapsed into unconsciousness. Brain surgery was performed to relieve swelling, but too much damage had been done. He died two days later.

Mark Donohue, one of the most intelligent drivers ever to run at Indy. He gave up a career in engineering to race professionally.

1973

High speed came with a high price at the 1973 Indy 500. With drivers coming tantalizingly close to 200 mph in practice, drivers were pushed to the limits of their capabilities. Veteran Art Pollard crashed in turn 1 with such force that his momentum carried him all the way into turn 2 before his crumpled wreckage stopped. He was already dead when help arrived. Rain postponed the race from Sunday to Monday, then tragedy struck again. As the pace car pulled off the track and the drivers gunned their way into the first lap, Salt Walther skidded and hit the wall. His fuel-laden car exploded, raining fuel on the crowd and badly burning 11 spectators. Eleven other cars got tangled up in the wreck, and the race was stopped. By the time the mess had been cleaned off the track, the rains came again and the 500 was postponed another day. Tuesday's start was also delayed by rain, and USAC officials decided to try again on Wednesday.

After more rain delays, the race finally began on Wednesday afternoon. Although the skies were dry, the track was not. This played havoc with the traction that the drivers needed to maneuver at high speeds. On lap 4, Pete Revson spun into the wall and was done for the day. Swede Savage, starting from the second row, assumed the lead after 40 laps of spirited jockeying between himself, Bobby Unser, Mark Donohue, and Gordon Johncock. Ten minutes later, Al Unser squeezed past Savage and into the lead. On lap 58, Savage lost control of his car, hit the outside wall in turn 4, then spun down the track, leaving a trail of fuel behind him. When he slammed into the inside wall, the entire track was engulfed in flames.

into the pits too aggressively and overshot his crew, which cost him precious time. Donohue suddenly had a three-lap lead over his nearest pursuer, Al Unser. He crossed the finish line in record time, the first Indy driver to average more than 160 mph.

Winner: Mark Donohue
Car: Sunoco McLaren
Speed: 162.9 mph
  2. Al Unser
  3. Joe Leonard
  4. Sam Sessions
  5. Sam Posey

Salt Walther's feet can be seen dangling from the wreckage of his car in the aftermath of the wreck that postponed the 1973 Indy 500.

Savage later died from burns and injuries, and a member of driver Graham McRae's pit crew was killed when he was hit by a fire truck speeding to the scene.

By the 100th lap, both Unsers were out with mechanical problems, and Donohue had a burned piston. This left Johncock all alone in front. Bill Vukovich, Jr. (the son of the 1950s star) slipped into second, but did not pose much of a threat to the leader. A half-hour later the rains returned and race officials, fearing more fatal wrecks, decided they had seen enough. Johncock was declared the winner after only 133 laps, but few at the Brickyard felt like celebrating.

Winner: Gordon Johncock
Car: STP Double Oil Filter
Speed: 159.0 mph
   2. Bill Vukovich, Jr.
   3. Roger McCluskey
   4. Mel Kenyon
   5. Gary Bettenhausen

1974

The horror show at Indy in 1973 prompted some major changes for 1974. The amount of fuel cars were allowed to carry was restricted to 40 gallons, and the gas tanks had to be located on the left side of the vehicle—toward the infield and away from the crowd. This meant cars would have to make six pit stops during the race, instead of four. Because a set of tires could be changed in the time it took to pump 40 gallons of gas, all of the teams switched to wider, softer, stickier tires for better traction. The tires wore down faster, but the extra fuel stops meant that they could swap them out without losing any time. USAC also aimed to reduce speed by forcing cars to use a special "pop-off" valve that would limit the power supplied by turbocharged engines. It was believed that A.J. Foyt, who had purchased Ford's racing factory after the company pulled out of the sport, would gain an unfair advantage from this rule. His engines were already designed to operate best at this new power level; the Offys that still propelled the majority of the cars at Indy were built to work most efficiently at much higher levels. When Foyt qualified with the highest speed—a "mere" 191.6 mph—it seemed that these suspicions were correct.

Of course, it takes a lot more than a good engine to win at the Brickyard. Foyt learned this the hard way, when he had to bow out of an early three-way duel for the lead after a slow pit stop. That left Johnny Rutherford and Bobby Unser to battle for first place. It took Foyt an hour, but he finally caught back up with the leaders and regained his advantage on the 138th lap.

A few minutes later, Foyt's engine began leaking oil. He saw the dreaded black flag, which meant he was being waved into the pits and, ultimately, out of the race. He watched helplessly as Rutherford and Unser roared away. Rutherford sensed that he had the better car on this day, and aimed to

prove it. He stomped on the gas pedal and wove through traffic hoping to shake Unser off his tail. This worked for a while, but in the final laps Unser crept back into contention. Rutherford, a Texan whose nickname was "Lonestar J-R," had never completed all 500 miles at Indy. On this day, he finally did it—just 22 seconds ahead of Unser, who had to settle for second place.

Winner: Johnny Rutherford
Car: McLaren
Speed: 158.6 mph
2. Bobby Unser
3. Bill Vukovich, Jr.
4. Gordon Johncock
5. David Hobbs

1975

Dan Gurney was an Indy legend. As a driver and owner, he had competed at the Brickyard for 14 years. And although Gurney had come close, he had never won. In 1975 he pinned his hopes on Bobby Unser, who qualified third. The top qualifier was A.J. Foyt, who had tasted victory three times, and was thirsty for a fourth triumph. Sitting in between them was Gordon Johncock, the 1973 winner. Johnny Rutherford, the defending champ, was poised to strike from the third row after qualifying seventh. The deck seemed stacked against an Unser-Gurney win.

Johncock's day ended just minutes after it began. He held first place briefly before an ignition problem knocked him out. Early ignition problems also eliminated Lloyd Ruby and Salt Walther—both of whom were among the fastest qualifiers. Wally

Dan Gurney displays the intense concentration that made him such a great competitor. He was an Indy pioneer as a driver and later as an owner.

Dallenbach, whose car was powered by a new engine designed by racing legends Art Sparks and Leo Goosen, put a charge into the crowd when he roared into the lead from 24th place.

Dallenbach was running the race of his life, keeping challengers Rutherford, Foyt, and Bobby Unser at bay, when he was forced to swerve down onto the grass to avoid a collision on Lap 162. This caused a slow leak in one of his tires, and he had no choice but to relinquish the lead. Unser, who had been running a steady, unspectacular race, saw Dallenbach's infield adventure and his eyes lit up. Now was his chance. With Gurney rooting him on from the pits, Unser powered into the lead when Rutherford refueled. After 174 laps, a sudden downpour ended the race. Unser took the checkered flag despite leading for no more than a few minutes

Winner: Bobby Unser
Car: Jorgensen Eagle
Speed: 149.2 mph
  2. Johnny Rutherford
  3. A. J. Foyt
  4. Pancho Carter
  5. Roger McCluskey

Bobby Unser poses in front of Dan Gurney's powder-blue Jorgensen-Eagle in 1975. Thanks to a rainstorm, Unser won the race after leading for just a few laps.

1976

The big news at the Brickyard during America's Bicentennial year was the presence of Janet Guthrie, the first woman ever to enter the race. Although she passed Indy's mandatory rookie test, her car developed mechanical problems. Practicing in A.J. Foyt's backup car, Guthrie got it up to 181 mph. But when qualifying came around, Foyt decided not to enter two cars in the race, and Guthrie was left without a ride. Meanwhile, in the year that had passed since the 1975 Indy 500, Johnny Rutherford had been unable to shake the gnawing feeling that he should have won that race. He vowed to do whatever was necessary to finish first this time.

When the green flag dropped, Rutherford charged to the head of the pack. Foyt quickly overtook him, then gave way to Pancho Carter. Wally Dallenbach and Gordon Johncock, both driving for the Patrick Racing Team, moved to the front next. They traded the lead a couple of times before Rutherford and Foyt reappeared to assume command. Foyt was slowed by steering problems, which opened the door for Rutherford on lap 80. By this time dark clouds were gathering, and a few minutes later a misty rain became a downpour. The red flag came out on lap 103, and the race was called off a few hours later. This time the rain had worked in Rutherford's favor. He was declared the winner of the shortest 500 ever, which lasted a grand total of 255 miles.

Winner: Johnny Rutherford
Car: Hy-Gain
Speed: 148.7 mph
  2. A. J. Foyt
  3. Gordon Johncock
  4. Wally Dallenbach
  5. Pancho Carter

Mario Andretti strikes a pose prior to the 1976 race. After winning the 500 in 1969, Andretti did not place among the Top 5 finishers again until 1981.

1977

After a disappointing race in 1976, fans flocked to the Brickyard expecting lots of excitement in 1977. They had reason to be optimistic. The track had been repaved, which meant speeds would be back up—and someone might even break the 200 mph barrier. Janet Guthrie had returned with a good car, Jimmy and James McElreath had a shot at becoming the first father-son driving combo in the starting grid, and A.J. Foyt—who had not won since 1967—had spent months preparing to win his fourth Indy 500. In the days leading up to the race, Guthrie qualified easily at 188 mph, Jimmy made it and James didn't, Foyt's high-powered Coyote looked terrific, and Tom Sneva ran two qualifying laps at 200 mph while winning the pole.

Al Unser led the race for the first 17 laps, with Gordon Johncock and Foyt close behind. Johncock overtook Unser, then gave way to Foyt, who relinquished the lead to Johncock 30 laps later. They raced together for the next 325 miles. Behind this duo, there was plenty of action. Defending champion Johnny Rutherford was the first driver out, with a valve problem. Guthrie lasted 27 laps before her engine died. Lloyd Ruby, in his 18th and final Indy, crashed into the wall on lap 35. Rookie Danny Ongais, frustrated by a long refueling stop, floored it out of the pits and ran a lap at the blinding speed of 192 mph.

With 20 laps to go, Johncock and Foyt both had to make one more pit stop. Their refueling times were roughly the same, enabling Johncock to maintain a slim advantage. On lap 184, however, Johncock busted his crankshaft and pulled off the track. A good sport, he waved to Foyt as he passed, congratulating him for a race well run. The

Four-time Indy winner A.J. Foyt. Some consider him to be the greatest all-around driver in the history of American auto racing.

Texan streaked across the finish line with his record-smashing win, then took a victory lap with ailing Tony Hulman aboard. The 76-year-old Hulman who resurrected the Speedway after World War II would not live out the year.

> **Winner: A. J. Foyt**
> Car: Coyote
> Speed: 161.3 mph
>   2. Tom Sneva
>   3. Al Unser
>   4. Wally Dallenbach
>   5. Johnny Parsons

1978

In the year leading up to the 1978 Indy 500, the biggest story in racing was A.J. Foyt's fourth win at the Brickyard. Among me-

The Cosworth engine, which came to dominate Indy racing in the late 1970s. Cosworth-powered cars won 10 races in a row at "The Brickyard."

chanics and engineers, however, the engine powering the cars right behind Foyt was the big story. Tom Sneva and Al Unser had used British-built Cosworth engines, as had Danny Ongais and Johnny Rutherford. The eye-opening performance of these Formula One motors had some whispering that the decades-long reign of the Offenhauser might be coming to an end. In 1978, one-third of the qualifiers used Cosworths, including the first five in the starting grid: Sneva, Ongais, Rick Mears, Rutherford, and Unser. Basically, they were blowing everyone off the track.

The early laps featured a tussle between Ongais and Sneva, with Unser joining this group, followed by Gordon Johncock. All four were running smoothly and staying out of trouble until lap 145, when Ongais started trailing smoke. He pulled into the pits and heard the bad news: he was done in by a blown engine.

Unser, who had put some space between himself and the other two, was in the perfect position to drive away with his third Indy victory. With 20 laps to go, he glided into the pits for a final splash of fuel—and ran over a loose tire! The damage to Unser's car was not enough to keep him off the track, but it was serious enough to warrant close attention. Luckily for him, Sneva had a lousy pit stop, too, and Johncock had dropped more than a lap off the pace by this time. Unser held his breath and drove carefully for the last 50 miles. He knew Sneva was closing fast, but estimated he could beat him to the finish line without pushing his car any harder. Unser was correct; he edged Sneva by a mere 8 seconds. Although Al had broken the Unser family "tie" with his third Indy win, the big story of the day was Janet Guthrie, who ran a magnificent race and finished ninth.

Janet Guthrie sits atop her historic 1977 entry. Any doubts about her talent were erased a year later, when she finished ninth.

> **Winner: Al Unser**
> Car: Lola
> Speed: 161.4 mph
> 2. Tom Sneva
> 3. Gordon Johncock
> 4. Steve Krisiloff
> 5. Wally Dallenbach

1979

The Indy 500 had become a cash machine during the 1970s. It generated countless millions of dollars for automotive companies, race sponsors, and television networks. In 1979, more than 100 cars entered the race, overwhelming the garage area and making qualifying even more hectic than usual. Given the amount of money and attention being focused on Indy, it was inevitable that, sooner or later, lawyers would get involved in the race.

This came to pass when USAC denied the entry applications of six drivers who had joined an organization called Championship Auto Racing Teams, or CART. CART was formed in 1978 by a group of racing people who felt that USAC was out of touch with the changing needs of drivers and team owners. Its founders meant to take control of the sport, and USAC knew it. CART staged Indy car events (15 in 1979) and already some of the top drivers had committed to race, including Wally Dallenbach, Gordon Johncock, Steve Krisiloff, Danny Ongais, and the Unser brothers.

These just happened to be the six drivers who were banned from the Indy 500 because they were not members "in good standing" with USAC. All were listed as "directors" in the new organization, so it was clear that

USAC needed to crush CART before it gained too much momentum. CART sued, claiming that USAC was denying its drivers a chance to make a living. The courts agreed, and ordered a special round of qualifying on the eve of the race so that the "CART Six" would have an opportunity to make the starting grid. The Unsers and Johncock qualified 3-4-5, Dallenbach 7th, and Ongais and Krisiloff started 27th and 28th, respectively. The pole-sitter, Rick Mears, was one of only three drivers to top 190 mph in qualifying.

No one was more relieved than the fans when the green flag dropped to start the race. They had paid a lot of money to sit in the stands, and all the last-minute legal maneuvering made them worry that the 500 would be postponed or cancelled. Al Unser sprinted to the front and set a blistering pace for the first 100 laps. Bobby Unser, A.J.

**The legendary Rick Mears,
who held off A.J. Foyt to take the
checkered flag in 1979.**

GREAT DRIVER: RICK MEARS

Rick Mears never wanted to draw attention to himself. He was quiet and shy, and never was a big fan of trophies and records. Beginning in his teen years, when he started racing motorcycles and dune buggies in California's Mojave Desert, he immersed himself in his sport.

Mear's driving skills and powers of concentration served him well during the 1977 season, his first behind the wheel of an Indy car. Although he failed to qualify for the 500 he ran several strong races that year. In 1978, the super-serious car owner Roger Penske hired the super-serious 26-year-old Mears to drive for his team. It was the start of one of the most successful owner-driver relationships in the history of racing.

In 1979, Mears took the pole at Indy and drove to victory. He won the 500 again in 1984, 1988, and 1991. He was also a three-time CART national champion, and the Associated Press Driver of the Decade for the 1980s.

What set Mears apart from his peers was his consistency, attention to detail, and his knowledge of the cars he drove. He got to know every nut, bolt, and weld, and would study computer printouts to help Penske engineers perfect his vehicle's handling. Confident of both his car and his abilities, Mears would wait for the perfect time to make his move in a race. Where other drivers took gambles, he took calculated risks. For this reason, Mears was among the most feared and respected competitors ever to compete at Indy.

Foyt, Tom Sneva, and Mears managed to stay close until a broken transmission seal finished Al's day. Bobby became the man to beat, and stayed ahead of Foyt and Mears for the next 200 miles. The race looked to be his until he lost his top gear and had to slow down. Mears took over on lap 182, and Foyt could not weave past the 15 cars between them to catch up. The man who had made a name for himself in off-road racing was the Indy 500 champ in just his second start.

Looking back, the USAC-CART rift could not have come at a worse time for the sport. The stock-car circuit, which was looked upon by Indy fans as "second-rate racing," was fast gaining in popularity. Earlier in the year, the Daytona 500 had been broadcast live on ABC for the first time and featured a wild finish that was tailor-made for television audiences. The new fans coming to auto racing would have a choice: NASCAR or Indy cars. Compared to USAC and CART, NASCAR was suddenly looking first-rate.

Winner: Rick Mears
Car: Gould Change
Speed: 158.9 mph
  2. A. J. Foyt
  3. Mike Mosley
  4. Danny Ongais
  5. Bobby Unser

CHAPTER 5

FAST TIMES

1980

For the first time in history, there were more similarities between Indy and Formula One cars than there were differences. The Offenhauser engine, which once seemed to offer engineers limitless possibilities, had all but given way to the high-powered Cosworth. The top seven finishers at Indy in 1979 used Cosworths; in 1980, there were 24 Cosworths in the starting grid to only three Offys.

Another European innovation was the "ground effects" strategy adopted by Indy racers. The use of air foils had become quite common at the Brickyard, but this was something more. Formula One designers had discovered that car bodies could be crafted to make the air flowing over and under the car exert a strong downward force— in effect, "nailing" it to the ground. That meant cars could maneuver quickly without skidding, and could take turns without slowing down. This led to tremendous controversy on the twisting, turning Grand Prix circuit, because it created some dangerous driving situations. Indy, on the other hand, was just one lefthand turn after another. All ground effects would do was improve the ride. Johnny Rutherford won the pole in a ground effects Chaparral; Mario Andretti and Bobby Unser sharing the front row with the two-time Indy winner.

Unser broke quickly at the start, before giving way to Gordon Johncock. Pancho Carter, Rutherford, Andretti, and Tom Sneva took turns in front, as the fans cheered the action. By the midway point, Andretti had dropped out, but defending champ Rick Mears joined the hunt.

With 40 laps left, Rutherford pitted. Mears and Sneva charged ahead, but Rutherford was coming up fast. His progress was thwarted when the yellow caution flag came out, but he renewed his attack when the race re-started. Rutherford flew past the leader, Sneva—who finished second for the third time in four years—and took the checkered flag by a good half-minute. After the race, Rutherford (who led for a total of 119 laps) was asked exactly when he knew he had the race won. Before it started, the Texan responded. Apparently a lady bug had come to rest on his arm prior to the parade lap. "I had always been told as a youngster that if a ladybug landed on you, it was a good-luck omen," he said. "I told my crew to load up and go home; we just won this thing."

GREAT DRIVER: JOHNNY RUTHERFORD

Sometimes success is just not in the stars. A driver can work all his life to become a champion, yet something always stands in his way. This certainly appeared to be the case with Johnny Rutherford, whose early career as an Indy car driver was fraught with misfortune and injury.

In 1963, the 25-year-old Rutherford earned his first start at the Brickyard but finished far off the pace after his transmission failed. In 1964, a crash ended his day. In 1965, he ran 15 laps before his transmission blew, and a year later he failed to qualify. Undaunted, Rutherford made the starting grid in 1967 only to crash midway through the race. In

1980 winner Johnny Rutherford waves to the fans. He credited a ladybug for supplying the luck he needed to win the race.

1968, he ruptured his oil tank during a wreck and had to withdraw. In 1969, the same thing happened.

The 1970s started off as badly as the 1960s. A broken header took Rutherford out of the 1970 race, and he was flagged for an oil leak in 1971. In 1972 he snapped a connecting rod. Things started looking up in 1973, when Rutherford established a new speed record in qualifying. But once again, lady luck frowned upon him and he was nine laps off the pace when the race was called because of rain.

After more than a decade of trying and failing, no one would have blamed Rutherford for quitting. But a switch to the hard-working McLaren team in 1973 convinced him that he finally had the right car and crew. He proved this in 1974— by not only finishing the race for the first time, but by winning it.

Rain ruined Rutherford's chances to win in 1975, but worked in his favor in 1976, when he edged out A.J. Foyt for his second Indy 500 victory. Rutherford won again in 1980, when engine power was reduced and new emphasis was placed on driver skill. It was the highlight of a spectacular season, during which he won four more major events and was crowned Indy car champion.

Rutherford's final triumph came at the Michigan 500 in 1986. At 48, he became the oldest Indy car driver to capture a 500-mile race. Despite a shaky start, Rutherford retired as one of the most popular people to ever compete at Indianapolis.

Winner: Johnny Rutherford
Car: Chaparral
Speed: 142.862 mph
  2. Tom Sneva
  3. Gary Bettenhausen
  4. Gordon Johncock
  5. Rick Mears

1981

For the first time since 1934, not one of the cars in the Indy 500 was powered by an Offenhauser engine. Cosworths took 12 of the first 14 starting spots—Mike Mosley, driving a Chevy-powered Eagle qualified second—and 29 of 33 overall. Meanwhile, the battle between USAC and CART moved from the courtroom to the track, where it belonged. Bobby Unser won the pole for CART with a qualifying speed of more than 200 mph. He shared the front row with Mosley and A.J. Foyt.

Unser controlled the race early, with Foyt and Gordon Johncock right behind him. Mosley, suffering from radiator problems, was out of the race after just a few minutes, but Rick Mears, Mario Andretti, Danny Ongais, and Tom Sneva were able to weave through traffic from the back rows and join the leaders. All spent time in front, as did Johncock, but the big surprise was rookie Josele Garza. The Mexican star dueled with Andretti and Johncock for 100 miles before a damaged suspension knocked him out of the race.

With 50 miles to go, Unser, Johncock, and Andretti were the men to beat. Johncock blew an engine with 18 laps to go, leaving Andretti to catch Unser alone. With Unser trying to conserve fuel, Andretti was able to pull within a few seconds of the leader. But after the checkered flag fell, it was Unser who was heading for Victory Lane.

Following the race, USAC announced that Unser was being penalized one lap for illegally passing during a caution period. That meant Andretti was the Indy winner. CART leader Roger Penske appealed the decision

Bobby Unser celebrates in Victory Lane after the 1981 race—his third win at Indy.

and four months later USAC reversed its decision. Unser had his third Indy championship, but not until he paid a fine of $40,000.

> **Winner: Bobby Unser**
> Car: The Norton Spirit
> Speed: 139.1 mph
>   2. Mario Andretti
>   3. Vern Schuppan
>   4. Kevin Cogan
>   5. Geoff Brabham

1982

Prize money in 1982 climbed to $2 million, and not surprisingly a record 109 drivers showed up at the Brickyard for qualifying. Of the 33 who made the cut, once again 29 had Cosworth engines. The British invasion was not limited to motors, however. More than half the car bodies in the race had been designed by the English auto maker March. The pole went to Rick Mears, with Kevin Cogan and A.J. Foyt (also driving a British-made March) sharing the front row. The pre-race runs were notable in that every car on the track was clearly capable of running at speeds above 200 mph. This may have led to the qualifying accident that took the life of Gordon Smiley. It was the first death at the Brickyard since 1973.

The race got off to a bad start when a first-lap accident took out Cogan, Mario Andretti, Roger Mears (Rick's brother), and Dale Whittington. Josele Garza, the surprising rookie of 1981, blew his engine on the restart, thinning the field to 28 cars. Foyt bolted to an early lead, with Mears challenging and Johncock right behind them. A fast pit stop enabled Tom Sneva to grab the lead

for 50 miles, but by the midway point Johncock was in the lead, with Mears, Sneva, and Pancho Carter a few seconds behind. Foyt, unable to solve a problem with his gear shift, called it a day on the after 94 laps.

With 40 laps to go, Sneva and Carter had faded, leaving Johncock in front, with Mears the only driver in position to catch him. Mears steadily closed the gap, and with just one lap to go he pulled even with Johncock. After failing to pass Johncock on the outside coming out of the final turn, Mears dipped inside and tried to catch the leader in an old-fashioned charge to the finish. Both cars roared across the line at more than 200 mph, with Johncock holding on by less than a car length to win.

> **Winner: Gordon Johncock**
> Car: STP Wildcat
> Speed: 162.0 mph
>   2. Rick Mears
>   3. Pancho Carter
>   4. Tom Sneva
>   5. Al Unser

1983

Often a bridesmaid, never a bride, Tom Sneva wanted an Indy win in the worst way. In 1982, he was running with the leaders late in the race when his engine failed. In 1977, 1978, and 1980, he finished second. After Sneva qualified fourth in 1983 with a blistering speed of 203.7 mph, his fans quietly wondered what would keep him out of Victory Lane this time. Fans of the Unsers had an extra reason to cheer this year, as Al Unser, Jr. made his first start at the Brickyard. Never before had a father and son run in the same Indy. The pole-winner, Teo Fabi, was a first-timer, too. He was far from a rookie, however, having starred on the Grand Prix circuit in Europe.

Fabi went in front early, but his day ended after less than an hour thanks to a bad fuel gasket. Sneva, Unser, Sr., Mike Mosley, Rick Mears, Geoff Brabham, and Bobby Rahal were all in the running at the midpoint, with Sneva pulling in front of Unser on lap 109.

On the 171st lap, Sneva's fans gasped when Mosley hit the wall right in front of him. Quick reflexes enabled the veteran to swerve around the accident and stay in the lead, but Unser, Sr. was able to take the lead after both drivers pitted under the caution flag. Six laps later, the green flag came out, and Unser, Jr.—several laps behind—positioned himself between his father and Sneva. This was not a legal maneuver, and official motioned for him to move out of Sneva's way. But the son continued to run interference for the father, as the laps melted away. Finally, on lap 190, the Unsers got stuck behind several other cars and had to slow down. In a daring move, Sneva accelerated and slipped underneath the two Unser cars to regain the lead. Unable to respond, Big Al finished second by 11 seconds, while Little Al ran out of gas. After a decade of attempts at the Brickyard, Sneva finally got to hoist the Borg-Warner trophy.

Winner: Tom Sneva
Car: Texaco Star
Speed: 162.1 mph
  2. Al Unser Sr.
  3. Rick Mears
  4. Geoff Brabham
  5. Kevin Cogan

1984

Long before the age of luxury skyboxes in baseball and football stadiums, the Indianapolis Motor Speedway built 27 trackside hospitality suites for the 1984 race. Corporate sponsors were flocking to Indy, plastering their decals on cars, sewing patches on drivers and crew members clothes, and buying billboards all over Indianapolis. Why not get a piece of that pie, Brickyard officials reasoned?

Champion Tom Sneva was the man everyone came to see, and he thrilled the crowd by breaking the 210 mph barrier in qualifying. However, there were other stories developing in the days before the big race. Emerson Fittipaldi, one of the greatest Formula One drivers in history, came out of retirement to try his hand at Indy. Roberto Guerrero, another Grand Prix star, was making his first Indy appearance, too. And the Unsers were joined by another father-son duo, as Mario and Michael Andretti occupied two spots on the second row of the starting grid.

It was Rick Mears, the third-fastest qualifier, who grabbed the early lead. The 1979 champion held the top spot until he pitted early on lap 25, allowing Sneva to pass him. Mario Andretti, setting a record pace, took over for several laps, before he was passed in the pits by Danny Ongais and Teo Fabi. These two fought it out briefly, until Sneva and Al Unser, Jr. gained the top two spots and waged a battle of their own. Little Al went out with a bad water pump and Mears reemerged to take the lead from Sneva, with Guerrero a full lap behind.

Sneva stayed on Mears's tail for nearly an hour, setting himself up for another win.

However, during a caution period, sparks began to fly from the rear of Sneva's car; a broken joint ended his day. With no one near him, Mears won the race without incident. The excitement was the result of the intense competition for spots 2 through 5. Al Unser, Sr. seemed to have second all wrapped up, until Guerrero—who had already had a collision and a spinout—started knocking down laps at 200-plus mph. He nipped Unser in the final stages, while two other rookies, Al Holbert and Michael Andretti, claimed the 4 and 5 spots. Mears's speed of 163.6 mph just missed breaking the record set by Mark Donohue 11 years earlier.

Winner: Rick Mears
Car: Pennzoil Z-7
Speed: 163.6 mph
  2. Roberto Guerrero
  3. Al Unser, Sr.
  4. Al Holbert
  5. Michael Andretti

1985

With CART playing an ever-growing role in the sport, prize money at Indy had doubled in less than five years. For the first time in 1985, the total purse was worth more than $3 million. This attracted a stellar qualifying field, and set the stage for a surprising challenge to the Cosworth engine. The two fastest qualifiers, Pancho Carter and Scott Brayton, were driving cars featuring a new Buick six-cylinder motor. They would have to fend off the likes of the Andrettis and Unsers, Rick Mears and Tom Sneva, and up-and-comers

Arie Luyendyk and Danny Sullivan—all of whom were driving Cosworth-powered Lolas, Marches, or Eagles. The old cliche "it's anybody's race" definitely applied at Indy in 1985.

Bobby Rahal, starting from the #3 spot, got in front of Carter in the early laps and stayed in front for a good half-hour. It turned out to be a short day for Carter; the pole-sitter was the first man out of the race, with a bad oil pump. Brayton retired 13 laps later with a bad cylinder. Thus a promising Indy for Buick had turned ugly in a hurry. Meanwhile, Mario Andretti and Emerson Fittipaldi caught up to Rahal, and then Sullivan passed all three.

By mid-race, Sullivan and Andretti were way out in front. Their wheel-to-wheel duel captivated the fans, especially after Sullivan spun out on the 120th lap, then somehow recovered to keep racing. By lap 176, when both drivers made a final pit stop, Sullivan had regained a slight advantage. He managed to hold this lead, even when Andretti mounted his final charge after a caution flag tightened the field with less than 10 miles to go. The margin of victory in Sullivan's "spin & win" was a mere 2.5 seconds. In third place, 10 seconds in back of Andretti, was Roberto Guerrero. It was the closest 1-2-3 finish in a long, long time.

Winner: Danny Sullivan
Car: Miller American
Speed: 153.0 mph
  2. Mario Andretti
  3. Roberto Guerrero
  4. Al Unser, Jr.
  5. Johnny Parsons

Danny Sullivan has the look of a man who can't quite believe his luck. He won the 1985 race after a miraculous recovery from a hair-raising spinout.

1986

The Indy 500 was 75 years old in 1986. As if to celebrate, the prize money rose to more than $4 million and the garage area—nicknamed "Gasoline Alley"—was completely redone. There was much anticipation as race day neared. Despite rules changes meant to slow everyone down, qualifying speeds climbed into the 210-215 mph range. Buick and Chevy had engines that they promised would give the Cosworth a run for the money, while Lola chassis were beginning to chip away at the dominance of March's. And after years of airing the race on tape delay, ABC finally decided to broadcast the 500 live.

Rain washed out the start of the race on Sunday and Monday, leading ABC to put off its live coverage until 1987. That was a shame, for this 500 was a superb one. Michael Andretti, starting third, beat pole-winner Rick Mears into the first turn. These two were joined by Bobby Rahal and Kevin Cogan, and by lap 49 they were well into a four-way battle that would last the rest of the day.

Mears grabbed the lead on the 135th lap and held it for an hour. On lap 186, Rahal passed Mears on the back straight, then Cogan nudged past Mears a lap later. An accident on lap 194 brought out the caution flag, and enabled Cogan to maintain his lead until the race re-started with less than three laps remaining. Realizing it was now or never, Rahal stomped on the gas the instant the green flag came out and got in front of Cogan—the 19th lead change of the day. The crowd watched in wonder as "Rapid Robert" circled the track at a record 209 mph and beat Cogan across the finish line by less than two seconds. Rahal, the first driver to complete the race in under three hours, drove down Victory Lane and onto a special raised podium that gave the crowd a great view of the winning wheel man and his car. Joining him there was Jim Trueman, the owner of Rahal's car. Nearly overcome with emotion, he stood with an ear to ear grin on his face. The win proved to be the crowning moment of his auto racing career. Two months later Trueman died of cancer.

Winner: Bobby Rahal
Car: Budweiser/Truesports
Speed: 170.7 mph
   2. **Kevin Cogan**
   3. **Rick Mears**
   4. **Roberto Guerrero**
   5. **Al Unser, Jr.**

Gasoline Alley, circa 1960. Indy fans would do anything for a chance to walk around this part of the track, which was renovated in 1986.

1987

Although big-time betting has never been part of the Indy 500, it is probably safe to say that the odds-makers did not factor Al Unser, Sr. into the outcome of the 1987 race. The veteran driver arrived at the Brickyard without a car, so no one was paying much attention to his presence there. But as practice and qualifying unfolded, it turned out that the three-time champion was in the right place at the right time. Danny Ongais, who bumped Unser off the Roger Penske team when he joined it over the winter, crashed in practice and suffered a concussion. Penske took a year-old chassis out of mothballs, dumped a new engine inside, and asked Unser to replace Ongais. He qualified 20th with a speed of 207.4 mph. Six rows in front of him were the three top qualifiers, Mario Andretti, Bobby Rahal,

and Rick Mears. Also in the starting field was Gordon Johncock—back from a two-year retirement—and Roberto Guerrero, who had yet to finish lower than fourth in any of his Indy starts.

As was his custom, Andretti burst into the lead and began to set a blazing pace. Guerrero briefly challenged him in the early stages, but a little over an hour into the race he and Danny Sullivan were almost a lap behind. Rahal and Mears, meanwhile, were plagued by mechanical problems and had already dropped out. At the midway point, Guerrero was the only one who looked like he had a chance to catch Andretti.

On lap 131 disaster struck. Tony Bettenhausen lost a wheel in turn 3, and Guerrero hit it at full speed. The tire sheared the nose cone off his March, then bounced into the crowd, where it killed a spectator. It had been 27 years since anyone had died in the stands at Indy. Guerrero was able to make repairs and get back on the track, but by this time Unser was creeping ever closer to second place. With 23 laps to go, Guerrero had a brief moment of good luck. Andretti, way out in front, pulled off the course with electrical problems. Sensing an easy win, Guerrero floored it and put almost two miles between himself and Unser. The bad luck returned six laps later, however, when his car stalled twice in the pits. Unser, playing the tortoise to Guerrero's hare, eased into first place. The Argentinian star tried desperately to make up the lap he lost, and was doing just that when the caution flag came out on lap 190. After four laps under the yellow flag, Guerrero found himself six cars behind Unser. In the final miles, he passed four of the six, but finished a frustrating second to the wily old-timer, who had run a perfect race.

> **Winner: Al Unser, Sr.**
> **Car: Cummins-Holset Turbos**
> **Speed: 162.175 mph**
>   2. Roberto Guerrero
>   3. Fabrizio Barbazza
>   4. Al Unser, Jr.
>   5. Gary Bettenhausen

1988

By 1988, the power shift from USAC to CART was complete. The sport was now run by the owners who risked their money and the drivers who risked their lives. The force behind this revolution had been Roger Penske, and in many ways the 1988 Indy 500 was an acknowledgement of all he had achieved. For the first time ever, all three cars in the front row belonged to one person. Rick Mears, Danny Sullivan, and Al Unser, Sr. were all driving for Penske Racing, and all three had turned in qualifying times over 215 mph. The dominance of the Penske cars and drivers made fans wonder whether anyone else had a chance to win the race.

With names like Arie Luyendyk, Emerson Fittipaldi, Roberto Guerrero, and Bobby Rahal, victory was far from assured for the Penske drivers. And the risk of a wreck always loomed. Indeed, Guerrero, Scott Brayton, and Tony Bettenhausen— three excellent drivers— all hit the wall in a turn 2 pileup before they had completed a single lap. Early accidents also ended the day for Teo Fabi, Tom Sneva, Ludwig Heimrath, and A.J. Foyt, Jr., who was driving for his dad's team in his third Indy start. Sure enough, just past the midway point, Sullivan grazed the wall and was out of the race.

That left Mears and Unser to battle it out. The two Penske drivers did just that until late in the race, when Fittipaldi, Michael Andretti, and Jim Crawford edged up on them. With 20 laps to go, Mears had a 15-second lead. With five laps to go he extended that bulge to a good 20 seconds over Fittipaldi, who by this time had nailed down second place. Penske watched with a mix of relief and satisfaction as Mears won a dangerous and chaotic race, while Unser finished a solid third. Penske cars led 192 of the 200 laps, and the victory was his team's fourth in five years. The folks at Chevrolet were happy, too. Their new engine took the top three spots, breaking Cosworth's 10-year winning streak.

Owner Roger Penske, who challenged the powers of Indy racing.

> **Winner: Rick Mears**
> Car: Pennzoil Z-7
> Speed: 144.8 mph
>   2. Emerson Fittipaldi
>   3. Al Unser, Sr.
>   6. Michael Andretti
>   5. Bobby Rahal

1989

When it was announced that the Speedway would get a fresh repaving after 12 years, fans flocked to qualifying to see if the 220 mph mark would fall. It did, thanks to Penske Racing's Rick Mears and Al Unser, Sr., who grabbed the first two spots in the front row with speeds over 223 mph. They would be vying for the first million-dollar winner's purse in Indy history, along with number-three qualifier Emerson Fittipaldi and Jim Crawford, Mario Andretti, and Scott Brayton, who made up the second row.

The first half of the race was not kind to Roger Penske's cars. Danny Sullivan was done in by a busted rear axle, and Unser retired with a bad clutch. Meanwhile, Andretti and his boy, Michael, each held the lead for several laps, marking the first time father and son had led the same race. A few laps into the second half, Penske's third car limped into the pits billowing smoke. Mears was through, with a blown engine.

With less than 50 laps to go, Fittipaldi, the younger Andretti, and Al Unser, Jr. were battling for the lead. Andretti's engine blew on lap 162, leaving Fittipaldi with a slim advantage. It took another 32 laps, but Unser, Jr. finally caught and passed Fittipaldi. On the next-to-last lap, Fittipaldi drew even and then the two cars bumped. Fittipaldi con-

Emerson Fittipaldi takes a break before race day. The Formula One legend "un-retired" to win Indy in 1989 and 1993.

trolled his vehicle but Unser, Jr. could not. He skidded into the wall, and the South American superstar took the final lap under caution. As Fittipaldi passed him on the way to the checkered flag, Little Al gave him a smile and a thumbs-up. It had been a great finish and both drivers knew it. Fittipaldi, a Formula One champion in 1972 at the age of 25, was the first foreign driver to win at Indy since 1966.

> **Winner: Emerson Fittipaldi**
> Car: Marlboro
> Speed: 167.6 mph
>   2. Al Unser, Jr.
>   3. Raul Boesel
>   4. Mario Andretti
>   5. A. J. Foyt, Jr.

1990

At the end of 1989, the Brickyard got a new boss. His name was Tony Hulman George, the grandson of the legendary Tony Hulman. He presided over a pre-race practice and qualifying period that saw Al Unser, Jr. complete a lap at more than 228 mph. Defending champion Emerson Fittipaldi took the pole, averaging 225.3 mph. He shared the front row with Rick Mears and Dutch star Arie Luyendyk, who had been driving in the U.S. for a decade and racing at Indy since 1985.

Fittipaldi got off to a roaring start. He stayed well ahead of his challengers, including Luyendyk, Mears, Bobby Rahal, and Unser, Jr. Not until his second pit stop did he relinquish the lead, and moments later he was back in front again. Fittipaldi was looking unstoppable until lap 135, when he made an unscheduled stop to change tires. It was an unusually cool day at the Brickyard, which was causing his tires to blister. Meanwhile, Rahal and Luyendyk, cruised past him.

Arie Luyendyk, who has enjoyed as close a relationship with "The Brickyard" as any modern driver.

With 50 laps to go, Fittipaldi's tires were giving him trouble again. The fans started to realize that Fittipaldi would not be winning this race. Their attention turned to Rahal, who was on pace to shatter the track record with an average speed over 180 mph. That is when Luyendyk began to close the gap. He took the lead on lap 167 and just flew around the track. By the time he took the checkered flag, Luyendyk had obliterated Rahal's 1986 record by 15 miles per hour.

Track owner Tony Hulman gives the traditional starting signal: "Gentlemen, start your engines."

Winner: Arie Luyendyk
Car: Domino's/Shierson Lola
Speed: 186.0 mph
   2. Bobby Rahal
   3. Emerson Fittipaldi
   4. Al Unser, Jr.
   5. Rick Mears

1991

The 1991 Indy 500 featured a fabulous first and a fond farewell. Willy T. Ribbs, an African-American, qualified 29th in a Buick-powered Lola owned by Walker Motorsports. Although he was by no means the first great black driver on the American auto racing scene, Ribbs was the first to make the starting field at Indy. This made for interesting pre-race copy, but it was nothing compared to the hoopla surrounding A.J. Foyt. After 34 consecutive years at the Brickyard, he announced that the 1991 race would be his last behind the wheel. Foyt claimed that racing was "passing him by." Then he went out and qualified second in a car he built himself at 222 mph! Foyt was joined on the front row by pole-winner Rick Mears and Mario Andretti. The event was a family affair for the Andretti clan. Besides Mario, Michael, John, and Jeff also made the starting grid. The defending champion, Arie Luyendyk, began the race back in the fifth row.

The day ended early for Ribbs when his engine blew on the fifth lap. Foyt was out 20 laps later with suspension problems. By then, Mario and Michael Andretti were out in front, with Emerson Fittipaldi coming up to challenge. "Emmo" grabbed the lead on lap 109, and for the next 60 laps he and Michael Andretti dueled for supremacy.

Meanwhile, Mears was making up ground on the leaders. After Fittipaldi bowed out with gear-box difficulties, Mears and Andretti were jockeying for position. Mears passed him on the 182nd lap, then Michael made a slick move to regain first place. Mears returned the favor and pulled into first as they entered the last 10 laps just a second or two apart. On lap 191, Mario Andretti's engine blew and the yellow caution flag came out. Both drivers knew it would be a sprint to the finish, and both hit the gas hard when the race resumed. Mears had a little bit more power, and beat Michael Andretti by a scant three seconds. He joined Al Unser and the retiring Foyt as the only four-time winners at Indy. As Mears's fans like to point out, their guy did it in 14 tries, while it took Foyt and Unser at least 20 years apiece.

Winner: Rick Mears
Car: Marlboro Penske
Speed: 176.5 mph
  2. Michael Andretti
  3. Arie Luyendyk
  4. Al Unser, Jr.
  5. John Andretti

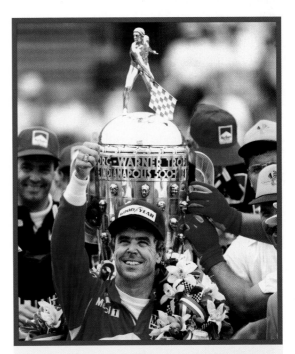

Rick Mears celebrates in front of the Borg-Warner Trophy after winning the 75th running of the Indy 500, in 1991.

1992

Coming off a big year, the Andrettis arrived at the Brickyard as the popular "first family" of Indy car racing. This did not sit too well with the Unsers; Al and Al, Jr. who had aimed to gain at least a share of this unofficial title in 1991. They were a few rows back when the race started, behind top qualifiers Roberto Guerrero, Eddie Cheever, and Mario Andretti. The last car to qualify was a Lola driven by Scott Goodyear. Normally, the #33 car does not figure into the outcome. But this was not a normal year. A.J. Foyt, disappointed by his early exit the previous year, came back and qualified 23rd. Jovy Marcelo, a rookie from the Philippines, crashed in qualifying and died from head injuries. He was the first driver in a decade to lose his life on the track. And Lyn St. James, a terrific and versatile veteran driver, became just the second woman to qualify for the 500.

It seemed only fitting in this out-of-the-ordinary atmosphere that something weird should happen even before the green flagged dropped. Race day was cold and overcast, and during the parade lap, pole-winner Guerrero decided to warm his tires. When he gunned his engine he lost control of his green-and-white Lola, which slammed into the wall. When the race finally started, Michael Andretti streaked in front from the second row, with his father and Cheever close behind. Carefully picking their way through the pack were the Unsers, with Goodyear moving up from last place as the race unfolded. Just before the midway point, Mario crashed on turn 1, leaving Michael to do battle with Cheever and Luyendyk, who had slipped quietly into contention. A half-hour later, Andretti was way out in front of Cheever and Luyendyk, and close to lapping

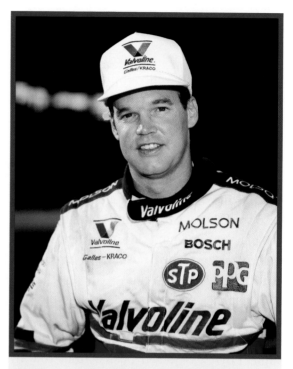

Al Unser, Jr., who made his Indy debut in 1983. He won the race in 1992 and again in 1994.

the fourth-place car, driven by Al Unser, Jr. On lap 136, Luyendyk and Foyt bumped, sending the Dutchman into the wall and out of the race. Al Unser, Sr. instantly became the fourth-place car, with his son moving past Cheever into second moments later.

Still, at this point it did not look like anyone could catch Michael Andretti. He was turning laps at close to 230 mph, and half the cars were gone from the race, which meant he had no traffic to slow him down. With 11 laps to go, the crowd gasped as Andretti slowed to an unexpected stop. After leading for more than 150 laps, he had fallen victim to a malfunctioning fuel pump.

All eyes now turned to Unser, Jr. and Goodyear, who were running neck-and-neck. Going into the final lap, they were

GREAT DRIVERS: THE UNSERS

The "first family" of the Indy 500 has to be the Unsers. Between Al, Bobby, and Al, Jr. they won the race an amazing nine times. Few fans know that the first Unser to run at Indy was Jerry, who died in 1959 after crashing during a test run at the Brickyard. Fewer still are aware that Jerry's twin, Louis, became a top engine-builder.

Bobby was the first to break through at Indy, winning the 500 in 1968. Al's flamboyant older brother won again in 1975 and 1981, making him the first three-decade champion. Al's first victory came in 1970, and he won again in 1971. After several off-years, Al won for a third time in 1978. Nine years later he took his fourth checkered flag at Indy.

The Unsers—Indy's most famous father-son duo.

By this time, Al, Jr. was busy making a name for himself. He won his first Indy car race in 1984 at the age of 22, and a year later lost the driving championship to his dad 151 points to 150. Al, Jr. won the Indy 500 in 1992, and again in 1994. He is still one of the sport's top drivers. The latest generation of Unsers includes Bobby's son, Robby, who won the Pike's Peak Hill Climb in 1990—the same race his dad won 13 times! And Jerry, Jr.'s son, Johnny, has found success on the IRL circuit.

Al, Jr. likes to say that his dad and uncle taught him everything he knows about racing, but is quick to add that—in this ultra-competitive family—they didn't teach him everything they knew. Who taught Bobby and Al, Jr.? Their father, Jerry Unser, Sr., was into racing but never got his name in the record books. However, Jerry's brother, Louie, was a big star in his day. Among his many victories were nine Pike's Peak championships.

still even. Goodyear seemed to gain an advantage when Unser's car wavered slightly, but a final burst of power gave Little Al the win by four one hundredths of a second. Al, Sr. crossed the finish line third behind these two, giving the Andretti family something to think about. As for St. James, she finished 11th—two spots behind Foyt—and was named Indy Rookie of the Year.

Winner: Al Unser, Jr.
Car: Valvoline Galmer
Speed: 134.5 mph
2. Scott Goodyear
3. Al Unser, Sr.
4. Eddie Cheever
5. Danny Sullivan

1993

The death of Jovy Marcelo and the appalling number of breakdowns at Indy in 1992 convinced officials to slow things down for 1993. Some subtle modifications to the track and to the cars driving on it did the trick, as qualifying speeds dipped down into the low 220s. This did not prevent the usual number of pre-race mishaps, which included a crash by stock-car specialist Robby Gordon, who was driving for A.J. Foyt. After the wreck, Foyt decided against racing again. He took a slow "farewell" lap instead, waving to the crowd in his famous #14 car. The Texan joined another four-time winner in retirement; Rick Mears had called it quits at the end of 1992.

In qualifying, Arie Luyendyk took the pole, with Mario Andretti and Raul Boesel sharing the front row. Emerson Fittipaldi, starting from the ninth spot, shared the third row with a fellow Formula One legend, Nigel Mansell. Two rows back was another Grand Prix superstar, Nelson Piquet. Also in this diverse starting field were Lyn St. James, Willy T. Ribbs, and Hiro Matsushita, the first Japanese driver to qualify for the 500.

Boesel took the early lead, but was penalized a lap when he illegally passed Mario Andretti during a caution period. A half-hour into the race, Al Unser, Sr. was in front. At 54, he was the oldest leader in race history. From there, the drivers played musical chairs at the head of the pack.

Early in the second half of the race, Mario Andretti seemed to be fashioning a good lead. But he was penalized for a violation in the pits, which opened the door for defending champion Al Unser, Jr. to grab first place. Thirty minutes later, Andretti caught Little Al and regained the lead. With 26 laps to go, Andretti still led, with Fitti-paldi and Mansell right behind him during a caution period. When the green flag dropped, Mansell darted past both cars and into the lead. Fittipaldi returned the favor 11 laps later, with a nice pass of his own. In the final minutes, Luyendyk took over second place after Mansell scraped the wall, however neither could catch Fittipaldi. He had led Indy for a mere 16 laps, but he was ahead when it counted.

> **Winner: Emerson Fittipaldi**
> Car: Marlboro Penske
> Speed: 157.2 mph
>   2. Arie Luyendyk
>   3. Nigel Mansell
>   4. Raul Boesel
>   5. Mario Andretti

1994

Emerson Fittipaldi's 1993 victory at Indy had been a triumph for team owner Roger Penske—who won for the ninth time at the Brickyard—and for the Chevy Indy engine, which had won for a sixth consecutive year. Penske was not one to rest on his laurels, however. He noted that the six cars finishing behind Fittipaldi all had the new Cosworth XB engine. In Penske's opinion, the Chevy's days were clearly numbered. Rather than buy Cosworths, he came to Indy in 1994 with powerful new Mercedes-Benz motors in cars driven by Fittipaldi, Al Unser, Jr., and Paul Tracy. For Unser, who qualified first with a speed of 228 mph, the days prior to the race were bittersweet. Shortly after they arrived at the Speedway, his father announced his retirement. Joining Unser in the front row were Raul Boesel and Fittipaldi.

Right behind them was an impressive young newcomer named Jacques Villenueve.

The two Penske drivers established an early lead, with Michael Andretti behind them. His father, Mario, took his first pit stop after 23 laps and never left. He was done for the day, courtesy of a bad fuel pump. After the race the superstar announced his retirement. Michael encountered some tire trouble, slipped back, and was replaced by Villenueve in third place.

Fittipaldi controlled the race for most of the day. With 15 laps to go, it looked like he would win for the second year in a row. Then, in an instant, a moment of carelessness or miscalculation cost Emmo the race. Roaring around turn 4, he drifted too high and slammed into the wall. Unser and Villenueve were left to fight for the victory, which went to Little Al. His Mercedes engine gave him the extra power he needed and delivered a record 10th victory to the Penske team.

Winner: Al Unser, Jr.
Car: Marlboro Penske
Speed: 160.9 mph
  2. Jacques Villenueve
  3. Bobby Rahal
  4. Jimmy Vasser
  5. Robby Gordon

1995

The 1995 Indy 500—the 50th presided over by the Hulman family—brought numerous changes to the sport. The Mercedes-Benz engine was gone, due to new rules from USAC. Teams that had committed themselves to this motor scrambled to bring new designs to the fore, with a Ford/Cosworth model leading

the way. Firestone, the tire company that had once dominated at Indy, returned to the Brickyard after a 20-year absence. Most teams had been riding on Goodyears, but Firestone aimed to break back into the business. The Indy Racing League (IRL)—a rival circuit to CART, founded by Speedway president Tony Hulman George—was getting geared up to start in 1996. Tom Binford, Indy's longtime chief track steward, would move into the IRL commissioner's office.

The race itself started with a bang, as Stan Fox swerved sharply from his spot on the fourth row seconds after the green flag came down. Fox's car hit the wall hard and disintegrated, leaving him strapped in his cockpit, fully exposed to the oncoming traffic. Though badly injured, he did survive. Three other drivers crashed in the ensuing pileup: Eddie Cheever, Lyn St. James, and Carlos Guerrero. Guerrero and St. James were both driving for Dick Simon Racing, leaving Simon with only one car and driver—Eliseo Salazar—still in the race. In front of this mess, Scott Goodyear zoomed ahead of pole-winner Scott Brayton. He was caught by Michael Andretti, who later gave way to Jacques Villenueve. But Villenueve was assessed a two-lap penalty for passing the pace car during a caution period. This looked like a race-killer for Villenueve, who was among the favorites when the day began.

An exciting newcomer to Indy racing, Mauricio Gugelmin, found the front of the pack to his liking. He and Goodyear dueled for almost 80 laps. Then Villenueve, who had quietly made up his penalty laps, reappeared and took over the top spot. With less than an hour to go, disaster again struck Villenueve. He stalled in the pits, and could only watch as Jimmy Vasser, Scott Pruett, and Goodyear all whizzed by. Vasser hit the wall on lap 170, giving Pruett the lead, but Goodyear pulled in front of Pruett soon after. When Pruett attempted to regain the lead, he skidded into the wall, too.

The wild day continued after Pruett's car was cleaned off the track. With Villenueve positioned right behind him, Goodyear wanted to get a quick start the instant the caution period ended. He gunned his engine too soon, however, and passed the pace car—just as Villenueve had earlier! Officials waved the black flag at Goodyear, instructing him to pull into the pits. Goodyear refused. He kept screaming around the track, far in front of Villenueve, who was now the official leader. A few minutes later, Villenueve crossed the finish line, with Christian Fittipaldi—Emerson's son—coming in second. Veteran Bobby Rahal finished third for the second straight year, while the stubborn Goodyear drew a five-lap penalty and was dropped down to 14th place. In a thrilling race—during which the leader was passed no fewer than 23 times—it was the passing of the pace car that decided the eventual victor.

> **Winner: Jacques Villenueve**
> Car: Player's LTD
> Speed: 153.6 mph
>   2. Christian Fittipaldi
>   3. Bobby Rahal
>   4. Eliseo Salazar
>   5. Robby Gordon

1996

"Star power" had long been the lure of the Indy 500, but in 1996 this was sadly lacking at the Speedway. Because of its close ties to the Brickyard, the IRL was guaranteed 25 of the 33 starting spots for its drivers. That left a lot of CART teams out in the cold. As a result, 17 first-time drivers qualified—most of whom were complete unknowns. In the race for the pole, Scott Brayton thrilled the crowd by turning in a record speed of 233.1 mph in his backup car. Six days later, Brayton was running practice laps when a rear tire suddenly deflated at full speed. He slammed into the wall and died. Tony Stewart, one of the 17 Indy rookies, assumed the pole position in Brayton's place.

Stewart looked like a veteran when the race started. He grabbed the lead and proceeded to turn the fastest lap in Indy history. Stewart was running fast, but he was not running smoothly. Nearing the midway point, his engine gave out and he was done for the day. A quartet of cars quickly moved in front, with Roberto Guerrero, Buddy Lazier, Davy Jones, and Eliseo Salazar vying for the lead.

Lazier held the lead until lap 120, when Guerrero passed him. Then Jones moved around him to take over second place. Guerrero and Jones raced 1-2 until Guerrero dropped back with a slow pit stop. With nine laps left, Lazier caught up with Jones. Two laps later he made his move and took command of the race. The final laps saw Jones try desperately to pass, but Lazier held him off to win.

> **Winner: Buddy Lazier**
> Car: Delta Faucet-Montana
> Speed: 147.9 mph
>   2. Davy Jones
>   3. Richie Hearn
>   4. Alessandro Zampedri
>   5. Roberto Guerrero

1997

Despite much criticism, the powers at Indy held their ground on the 25-8 rule favoring IRL drivers. Once again, many CART teams boycotted the race. And as expected, the starting field was full of rookies—13 to be exact. At least the pole-winner was familiar to fans at the Brickyard. Arie Luyendyk, the 1990 winner, grabbed the first spot with a speed of 218 mph. However, compared to past years, this was not an awe-inspiring speed. Clearly, this was anyone's race.

The start, delayed a day by rain, was a sloppy one. Before the green flag dropped, an accident had wiped out three cars, and two others had limped into the pits with race-ending mechanical problems. When the smoke finally cleared, Tony Stewart built a slight edge over Luyendyk. On lap 15, the rains came again and the race was postponed another day.

When the race resumed the next day, Stewart protected his lead over Luyendyk for another 50 laps, before the Dutchman overtook him. Luyendyk held the top spot until just after the midway point of the race. After that, for most of the second half, the race leader was rookie Jeff Ward. He was followed closely by Luyendyk, Stewart, Scott Goodyear, and defending champion, Buddy Lazier. Low on fuel, Ward decided to pit for a "splash & go," but while he did Goodyear and Luyendyk—teammates on the Treadway Racing team—sped past him. Two laps later, Luyendyk took the lead. Two laps after that, one of Lazier's mirrors flew off and the yellow caution flag came out.

This is when things got a little weird. The race restarted on lap 198, only to stop again moments later when Stewart brushed against the wall. Everyone assumed the race would finish under caution, but when cleanup crews could find no debris, the green flag was waved. This caught most of the drivers off guard, because the track lights still flashed yellow. Luyendyk noticed the flag a heartbeat before Goodyear, who was directly behind him. He slammed on the gas and beat his teammate to the checkered flag by less than a second.

Winner: Arie Luyendyk
Car: G-Force
Speed: 145.8 mph
2. Scott Goodyear
3. Jeff Ward
4. Buddy Lazier
5. Tony Stewart

1998

By 1998 it had become clear that no one was going to "win" the battle between the IRL and CART. And if something wasn't done to mend fences, the biggest loser was going to be the Indy 500. Although attendance and sponsorship money continued to be strong, public interest in the event was starting to diminish. Casual auto racing fans were confused by the conflict, and many switched their allegiance to NASCAR. To remedy this the 25-8 rule was discarded and an uneasy truce was called for the Brickyard. The result was increased excitement in qualifying, and a starting field full of stars, including Tony Stewart, Greg Ray, Kenny Brack, Buddy Lazier, Eddie Cheever, Arie Luyendyk, and pole-winner Billy Boat. Also among the starters was rookie Robbie Unser, the third generation of the Unser family to race at Indy.

Rain, an accident, and a stray dog delayed the action, but once the race began it was a good one. Boat zoomed along in front for 13 laps, before Ray took the lead. Stewart was in the mix, too, until engine problems forced him out. Brack spent a good portion of the race out front, while Luyendyk, Unser, and Cheever challenged.

On lap 151, the picture got a little clearer. Cheever passed Brack and Luyendyk's car died in the pits. Ray also retired with mechanical troubles, leaving Lazier as Cheever's lone challenger. In the final 10 laps, Lazier had his chances, but Cheever proved too tough. Cheever hung on for the victory.

> **Winner: Eddie Cheever**
> Car: Dallara
> Speed: 145.155 mph
>   2. Buddy Lazier
>   3. Steve Knapp
>   4. Davey Hamilton
>   5. Robbie Unser

1999

It had been six years since A.J. Foyt drove his last race at the Brickyard, and 22 years since his last visit to Victory Lane. Now a respected team owner, Foyt was pinning his hopes on Kenny Brack, the Swedish star who had led for much of the 1998 race, and Billy Boat, the previous year's pole-winner. In qualifying, however, it was Arie Luyendyk who established himself as the man to beat. The two-time winner announced that this race would be his last; he was retiring from racing at the end of the year. Robby Gordon, Jeff Ward, and Greg Ray also looked good in the days before the race.

Luyendyk did not disappoint his fans, as he led for the first 32 laps. Ray kept him in sight the whole time, with Brack and Boat hanging back, just off the pace. Their patience paid off when Luyendyk and Ray both crashed. Gordon and Ward joined the leaders, and for more than 100 laps the race was completely up for grabs.

By lap 164, Gordon had established a solid lead. But as the race wound down, he could not shake his pursuers. Fearing he would lose the lead for good if he pitted for a final fuel stop, Gordon decided to gamble that he had enough left in his tank to finish the race and just kept going. In the pits, Foyt did not need a calculator to do the math. He told Brack that Gordon would have to pit, and advised him to nail down second place and wait. Brack pulled ahead of Ward and into second place. With 11 laps left, Gordon faced the fact that he would not be able to finish with what he had. He zoomed into the pits for a few gallons of gas and then got right back out, but Brack, Ward, and Boat had gotten past him. That is how the quartet finished a few minutes later, as Foyt literally jumped for joy before heading toward Victory Lane.

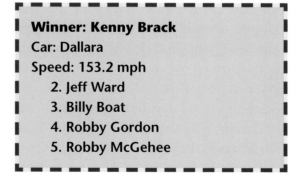

> **Winner: Kenny Brack**
> Car: Dallara
> Speed: 153.2 mph
>   2. Jeff Ward
>   3. Billy Boat
>   4. Robby Gordon
>   5. Robby McGehee

2000

In 2000, the final olive branch was passed between the rival racing leagues when Chip

GREAT DRIVER: ARIE LUYENDYK

Has there ever been a driver who loved the Indy 500 more than Dutch star Arie Luyendyk? It was at the Brickyard in 1990—at the age of 36 and after seven winless years on the circuit—that he finally broke through by edging Bobby Rahal and obliterating the old speed mark by 15 mph. Prior to that day, he was known as "Lightfoot" Luyendyk because he rarely jammed on the gas and took chances.

With a new reputation and better cars to drive, Luyendyk finished his career with a flourish and won back the respect of his fans and his racing peers. He captured the Indy crown again in 1997, then retired in 1999. Two years later Luyendyk was back at the Brickyard looking for a third victory. He finished 13th, but had the time of his life.

Arie Luyendyk's 1990 victory ranks among history's most impressive. He obliterated the old speed mark by 15 mph.

Now known as the "Flying Dutchman," Luyendyk decided to make Indy the only race he runs, and plans to un-retire each spring until they will have him no more. By that time his son, Arie, Jr., will probably be ready to take his place. In 2002 the 20-year-old began his first season in the Indy Racing League.

Ganassi, owner of CART's top racing team, agreed to race at the Brickyard. His best driver, Juan Montoya, could not wait to get his first crack at Indy. However, it was an IRL driver, Greg Ray, who stole all the headlines when he won the pole at 223 mph.

Ray opened the race running strong, and led for 26 laps. He gave way to the hard-charging Montoya, who was later passed by teammate Jimmy Vasser and Robby McGehee. It did not take long for Montoya to find his way back into the lead. The Colombian superstar was in command for the next 140 laps, with Vasser and Buddy Lazier giving chase.

The only shaky moment for Montoya came when Vasser grabbed first during a pit stop. But on lap 180, Montoya took control of the race for good, as Vasser dropped back and the new second-place car, driven by Lazier, was too far off the pace. Minutes later Montoya took the checkered flag—the first rookie to do so since Graham Hill in 1966. After the race, CART people made a big deal out of Montoya's dominant performance. But most Indy fans were just happy that all of the sport's best drivers were finally back at the Brickyard, settling their differences on the track instead of in the courtroom.

```
Winner: Juan Montoya
Car: G-Force
Speed: 167.5 mph
    2. Buddy Lazier
    3. Eliseo Salazar
    4. Jeff Ward
    5. Eddie Cheever, Jr.
```

2001

Just as Indy got its house in order, racing critics launched a new attack on the 500. The Brickyard was "missing something," they said, the old-time enthusiasm and over-the-top personalities were just not there anymore. Some blamed the incredible technology that had come to auto racing—a driver was just like a part of the car now. Into this negative atmosphere came a couple of Brazilians named Helio Castroneves and Gil de Ferran. They worked for Roger Penske, and they were not your typical drivers. They loved to race; it was obvious in everything they said and did. The Brazilians were up against pole winner Scott Sharp, who notched a speed of 226 mph in qualifying, as well as Michael Andretti, Greg Ray and Robbie Buhl—each of whom was considered a threat to take the checkered flag. Arie Luyendyk, who came out of retirement, was also given a good chance to win.

Three accidents in the first 17 laps made a mess of the early stages, with Sharp the most notable casualty. Ray and Andretti dueled for the lead until Luyendyk passed them both. It was not until midway through the race that the Brazilian drivers began to move on the leaders. Castroneves and de Ferran surged in front as Ray dropped back. Buhl and Andretti remained in the hunt. With the skies threatening, no one seemed to be able to take firm command of the race. Just as Castroneves managed to open a slight lead, the race was halted because of rain. The leaders were on the 149th lap.

When the action resumed, de Ferran mounted a challenge to Castroneves, but lost momentum when a spinout by Buhl brought out the caution flag. On the re-start, de Ferran actually pulled even with his fellow Brazilian for a moment, but Castroneves jammed on the accelerator and left his countryman behind. Not until lap 199 did de Ferran get close again. By that time, there were too many cars between him and Castroneves to make a final pass.

Castroneves took a victory lap and then parked his car on the finish line. He leaped onto the pavement, sprinted to the wire screen separating the grandstand from the track, and scrambled his way up like Spiderman, pumping his fist in triumph. Castroneves and the Penske pit crew then threw one of the wildest, most spontaneous celebrations in Brickyard history. Needless to say, no one leaving Indy that day was wondering where the old-time enthusiasm had gone.

```
Winner: Helio Castroneves
Car: Dallara
Speed: 153.6 mph
    2. Gil de Ferran
    3. Michael Andretti
    4. Jimmy Vasser
    5. Bruno Junqueira
```

2002

The hot topic at Indy in 2002 was the installation of new "soft" walls engineered to lessen the severity of crashes. The hot rookie was Tomas Scheckter. And the hot car belonged to pole-winner Bruno Junqueira. Expected to give these two a run for their money were Gil de Ferran, reigning IRL champion Sam Hornish, NASCAR's Tony Stewart, rookie Dario Franchitti, and Kenny Brack, who was returning to the Brickyard for the first time since winning in 1999. In truth, there were at least 15 drivers with a legitimate shot at the checkered flag. Defending champion Helio Castroneves did not consider himself to be part of this group. Although he was a supremely talented oval-track driver, for this race he felt his car lacked the power to take the checkered flag. His strategy was to drive conservatively, stay out of trouble, and just finish the race.

It was an exciting day that featured 19 lead changes and 9 leaders, as well as five potentially serious accidents. The new walls did their job, however, as the worst injury suffered on this day was a concussion. Two of the crashes were of the rarest variety: one-car wrecks involving the race leader. The first came on lap 87, when Junqueira blew his gear box. The oil from this mishap caused the race's early leader, Tony Kanaan, to spin out and hit the wall.

As the race passed the midway point, Scheckter began to establish himself as the man to beat. He seemed to be in command with less than 100 miles to go, but on lap 173 he came out of turn 4 a bit too fast and slammed into the wall. This gave de Ferran first place. He and others in the lead pack pitted during the caution for a final splash of fuel and new tires. But on the way out, one

of de Ferran's tires rolled off. When the caution was lifted, Castroneves—who chose not to pit—grabbed first place with 23 laps left.

The fans cheered the 2001 race winner, not realizing that he lacked the fuel to finish at full speed. Castroneves's only hope was to hold off hard-charging Paul Tracy, and pray for a yellow flag to appear. Incredibly, with less than two laps to go, Buddy Lazier and Laurent Redon—well back in the pack—crashed an instant before Tracy shot past Castroneves. The caution flag came out and the Brazilian slowed down, conserving the last few drops of gas in his tank. A frustrated Tracy (who claimed he did not see the yellow) was forced to accept a second-place finish. This time when Castroneves climbed the screen in front of the grandstand, he was joined by his entire pit crew.

Winner: Helio Castroneves
Car: Chevrolet
Speed: 166.5 mph
    2. Paul Tracy
    3. Felipe Giaffone
    4. Alex Barron
    5. Eddie Cheever

As the Indianapolis 500 closes in on its 100th birthday, we can look back on good times, bad times, and troubling times. Through it all, however, the race has served as a vivid reminder of man's unrelenting quest for speed.

When Indy fans look ahead, what do they see? The picture is not clear. It is hard to imagine a Memorial Day weekend without a 500-mile race at the Brickyard, but there is no denying that interest in the event has waned in recent years. Although the

Indy 500 remains as one of the most coveted tickets in all of sports, television ratings are down and so is overall interest.

When the Indy Racing League was formed in 1996 to go head-to-head with CART, it caused confusion among racing fans. The public relations battles waged between the two organizations also left fans with the impression that neither circuit had any true superstars. As a result, by the time the Indy 500 rolls around each spring, there are no "marquee" drivers to pull fans into the event.

So what is the 500 to do?

It must put the brakes on the bickering once and for all.

In fact, the sport should actually celebrate the differences between IRL and CART, which would put the drivers in the spotlight once again. IRL races are held on oval tracks, like the Speedway, while the majority of CART events are now road races. Each type of driving demands incredible skill and daring, and each circuit has a cast of colorful characters to root for.

It doesn't take a genius to see that people would much rather watch a showdown between the superstars of CART and IRL than to listen to a bunch of bickering lawyers and racing executives. Indeed, by working closely with CART, and marketing itself wisely, the Indy 500 should be able to make up all of the ground it has lost, and then some…and recapture its past glory just in time to kick off a second century of great racing.

2003

With Helio Castroneves and Gil de Ferran driving for him, team owner Roger Penske had reason to be optimistic about his chances of winning the Indianapolis 500 for a record

2001 Indy champion Helio Castroneves lives up to his nickname: "The Spider."

13th time. Castroneves, bidding to become the first driver to win three consecutive races at the Brickyard, was the odds-on favorite, while de Ferran figured to be among the leaders if everything went according to plan.

While Castroneves had won in his only two visits to Indy, Michael Andretti had been chasing the checkered flag since 1984. He planned to retire at season's end, and hoped his run of bad luck and near misses might come to an end. In the race's early stages, Andretti did indeed work his way to the front of the pack, and led for 28 laps before engine trouble finished his day. The good news was that three Andretti-owned cars—driven by Tony Kanaan, Robby Gordon and rookie Dan Wheldon—were all within striking distance of the new leader, Castroneves.

For the next 100-plus laps, the lead changed hands several times, with Castroneves, de Ferran, Kanaan, and Tomas Scheckter taking turns in front of the pack. On lap 167, the two leaders pitted simultaneously, with de Ferran maintaining his slim lead. Castroneves slipped past him, but with 31 laps to go de Ferran skillfully used a slower car driven by A.J. Foyt V to block Castroneves and charge into the lead.

Lap 187 saw the most dramatic crash of the day, as Wheldon tried to stave off a challenge by Sam Hornish, Jr. He forced Hornish toward the grass as the two cars screamed down the backstretch, but to Wheldon's horror he realized that he was running too fast and too low to negotiate Turn 3. He slammed into the wall and flipped over, but somehow managed to walk away from the wreck. The final laps came down to a duel between the two Brazilians, with de Ferran maintaining his razor-thin lead. Castroneves never gave up, finishing less than a second behind his teammate.

Winner: Gil de Ferran
Car: G-Force
Speed: 156.3 mph
   2. Helio Castroneves, Dallara
   3. Tony Kanaan, Dallara
   4. Tomas Scheckter, G-Force
   5. Tora Tagaki, G-Force

For More Information

Guzzardi, Giuseppe and Rizzo, Enzo. *The Century of Motor Racing.* Vercelli, Italy: White Star S.r.l., 1999.

Owen, Dan. *Vintage & Historic Indianapolis Race Cars.* Osceola, Wisconsin: MBI Publishing Company, 1998.

Popley, Rick. *Indianapolis 500 Chronicle.* Lincolnwood, Illinois: Publications International Ltd., 1998.

Rendall, Ivan. *The Chequered Flag.* London, England: Weidenfeld & Nicolson, 1993.

Stewart, Mark: *Auto Racing.* Danbury, Conneticut: Franklin Watts, 1998.

Taylor, Rich. *Indy: 75 Years of Racing's Greatest Spectacle.* New York: St. Martin's Press, 1991.

Index

Page numbers in *italics* indicate illustrations.

About the Author

Mark Stewart ranks among the busiest sportswriters today. He has produced hundreds of profiles on athletes past and present and has authored more than 80 books, including all titles in **The Watts History of Sports.** A graduate of Duke University, Stewart is currently president of Team Stewart, Inc., a sports information and resource company in New Jersey.